DAVID A. CASTRO

understanding
voices, noises & presences
in the spiritual realm

Understanding Voices, Noises & Presences in the Spiritual Realm

Published by: *David A. Castro* Brooklyn, New York
www.brooklynblessing.com   www.twitter.com/daword

Purchase online from: www.Amazon.com

Printed in the United States of America

International Standard Book Number: 0-9637001-4-6

Library of Congress Catalog Card Number: 93-90286

TABLE OF CONTENTS

INTRODUCTION

Psalms 46:10a Be still, and know that I am God.

Be still. Oh what a challenge. The business of life requires so much of our attention, constantly. There is so much commotion and activity in the world. Yet, with all of our natural responsibilities and doings, the Lord still commands us to, "Be still." He knows that it is then, and only then, that we will be able to get to know Him—His ways, His moods, His leadings.

When we learn to be still in His presence, we will be able to perceive the several manifestations of His Spirit by which He may be pleased to visit us. The inner witness of His Spirit, the still, small voice of His Spirit, and the diversities of impressions of His Spirit, will then be more pronounced and clear to us. The presences of angels, special anointings, and the audible voice of God, will also be easier for us to perceive when we have quieted our souls and stilled our bodies in His presence.

Throughout the Bible, there are many exhortations from the Lord for us to be sensitive to Him, to yield to Him, to seek Him, to wholeheartedly give ourselves unto Him. And in the Bible there are also many instances in which God showed up in a great and mighty way when His people obeyed the exhortations.

Exodus 17:6 Behold, I will stand before thee there upon the rock In Horeb; and thou shalt smite the rock, and there shall come water out of it, that the people may drink. And Moses did so in the sight of the elders of Israel.

In the time of Israel's wanderings in the wilderness, God told Moses to smite the rock in Horeb so that water may come out of it and the people may drink.

In His instruction to Moses, God had said, "I will stand before thee *there* upon the rock." God was not standing on the other side of the rock, or in the field. He was standing in a specific place, at a specific time, for a specific purpose. As Moses got in concert with God's presence, and yielded to His leading, the Lord (represented by, and present in, that *Rock* which is *Christ;* 1Corinthians 10:4) was able to miraculously produce water from the rock.

We, too, can receive a leading from God to do a certain thing, at a certain time, in a certain place, and find God standing there with our miracle. Many times, the Lord will tell a person who is sitting in Church to come up to the altar and God will *meet him there.* Or He will tell a person to go into his prayer room and God will bless him *there.* He may also tell a person to stay away from a certain place—a house, a Church, a store, or even a person—because His presence is peculiarly absent *there.*

Voices, noises, and presences in the spiritual realm, may or may not be of God, and in the following pages we will attempt to examine both good and evil ones. As we learn how to yield to the Spirit of God, He will, at times, open up a realm and encourage us to enter it. He will enable us to be spiritually sensitive so that we can perceive activity there, perceive Him, and receive of Him a special manifestation. A response to our prayers, a healing for our bodies, answers to our questions, and other needs which we may have, can be met by the Holy Spirit as He visits us, and as we yield to His visitation.

Many things are always happening in the realm of the spirit. Although the Lord will not disclose everything to us that we would like to know, a great many things which we have longed for and required, which have been hid from our eyes, can be found in His presence when we are still and silent before Him. And this doesn't mean that we need to abandon or neglect the natural responsibilities of our lives.

Colossians 3:1-2 If ye then be risen with Christ, seek those things which

are above, where Christ sitteth on the right hand of God. Set your affection on things above, not on things on the earth.

As Christians, we should take the liberty and confidence to walk in the spirit, to be spiritually-minded, and to be in tune with the doings of the Spirit of God. The Apostle Paul exhorts us to seek those things which are above this natural plane. Though we will often be tempted to fear that higher plane because it may be strange to us, we have the assurance that our Jesus will show up in the midst and tell us, "It is I, be not afraid."

This has been my experience over the last few years. As I have sought the Lord, I have found Him. As I have yielded to His Spirit, I have encountered Him. As I have sought to understand manifestations of the Holy Spirit, and the spiritual realm in general, I have learned and experienced a few things. And as God has desired to visit, and reveal, and manifest Himself unto His people, I have occasionally received wonderful manifestations of Him.

As you ask, you, too, shall receive. As you seek, you, too, shall find. As you knock, unto you, too, shall the windows of Heaven be opened.

The windows of Heaven are open. The rains of God's Spirit are falling. Ho, everyone that thirsts, come to the waters. Drink freely. Be ye filled. Whosoever will, take the water of life freely.

Reader, read on. Drink on. Press on. Go on to higher heights and deeper depths of the Word and of the Spirit of God. Angels, authorities, powers, and all other spirits as well, are subject unto Jesus Christ, the Lord of all. Therefore, no weapon that is formed against you shall prosper. Fear not, but have faith for the supernatural. In Jesus' Name.

Chapter 1

YIELD TO THE SPIRIT

1Corinthians 14:10 There are, it may be, so many kinds of voices in the world, and none of them is without signification.

There are many kinds of *voices* in the world. In Greek, the word is *phone,* and it means, "voice, noise, sound, tone, or utterance." There are three heavens, and many kinds of beings and activities in each. Therefore, an innumerable variety of utterances and sounds are made throughout, and they all have their significance. Something's in the air, and an attentive ear can occasionally pick up a significant sound. Even inanimate objects make sounds which can be heard, and they, too, may have distinct meanings.

1Corinthians 14:7 And even things without life giving sound...

Spiritual, invisible things are not seeable except by a supernatural disclosure from God. Similarly, voices and sounds which are not in the natural realm cannot be heard unless the Lord opens our ears to them. However, once our ears have been opened to the spiritual realm, they can become sensitive to hear things in the spirit without God having to open them supernaturally each and every time He wants us to hear something there. When we live naturally in the spirit, we can communicate naturally in the spirit.

We can learn how to see some things which are in the realm of the spirit in addition to those things which God would disclose supernaturally. We may also hear voices or sounds as God directly discloses something to us. Or, as we simply enter the realm of the spirit by faith, we might hear words or sounds which are already there, without a specific message from God being disclosed to us. By consciously acknowledging the spiritual realm around us, and by prayerfully giving our attention to it, we are exercising our spiritual senses and our spiritual gifts, and it gradually becomes easier and easier to discern what's happening there. This is the way we train ourselves in spiritual things. This is the way the spiritual realm becomes less strange or threatening.

Hebrews 5:14 But strong meat belongeth to them that are of full age, even those who by reason of use have their senses exercised to discern both good and evil.

Our eyes, by reason of use, can become trained to discern spiritual sights, therefore, our ears can also become trained to discern spiritual sounds. Many principles of learning which apply to *visual disclosings* apply to *audible* and *tangible* ones as well.

Supernatural experiences are usually characterized by *voices, noises* or *presences* of some kind. A supernatural experience may begin with a small degree of these in order to lead us to a greater manifestation of the Holy Spirit. Spectacular visions are often preceded by spiritual sounds and/or presences. Therefore, we may train all our senses to discern and respond appropriately to them.

In St. John's visit to Heaven (Revelation 1-4), he experienced a gradually increasing revelation from the Lord. He first heard the voice of the Lord (1:10-11), then saw visions (1:12-16), then fell into a trance (1:17), and finally was taken up by the Spirit of the Lord to behold the Throne of God, (4:1-2). That he was alone on Patmos Island helped him to be still before the Lord and get to know his God more intimately, and probably helped make him more conducive to apprehend deep spiritual insights. Sometimes we need to come aside and be alone with God before He really speaks to us by powerful visions.

On many occasions, I, too, have perceived a special presence before going into a supernatural dream, trance, or out-of-body experience. Such a presence can be characterized by a variety of manifestations, even unpleasant ones. If we would only be still, and not be easily moved or disturbed by an unfamiliar presence, we might find a special visitation of the Lord hiding behind the seeming darkness, as did many of His servants in the Bible.

The Patriarch Abraham experienced a *horror of great darkness* that *fell upon him* in a trance from the Lord, (Genesis 15:12). The Prophet Isaiah felt *undone.* He became so frightened at the visitation of God, that he thought he was going to die, (Isaiah 6:5). The Prophet Daniel was *grieved in his spirit in the midst of his body* (Daniel 7:15); was *much troubled* (Daniel 7:28); experienced *corruption* (Daniel 10:8); and *fainted* and was *sick certain days* at the astonishing visitations of God, (Daniel 8:27). Daniel's friends also experienced a visitation from God, but they couldn't endure the *great quaking* which *fell upon them,* so they fled to hide themselves, (Daniel 10:7). Now consider one of Job's friends:

Job 4:12-16 Now a thing was secretly brought to me, and mine ear received a little thereof. In thoughts from the visions of the night, when deep sleep falleth on men, Fear came upon me, and trembling, which made all my bones to shake. Then a spirit passed before my face; the hair of my flesh stood up: It stood still, but I could not discern the form thereof: an image was before mine eyes, there was silence, and I heard a voice, saying.

Job's friend, Eliphaz, was secretly visited by an angel of the Lord. Here, too, the messenger came with a gradually increasing presence: first in *dream-thoughts,* then in a *deep sleep* with *trembling,* then a *spirit passing* before his face, then an *image appearing* before his eyes, and finally a *voice speaking* a revelation from the Lord, (verses 17-21). That he received only "a little thereof" implies that he could have received more if he would have yielded more. Perhaps his fear robbed him of a portion of what was being disclosed.

Job 4:15 (tev) A light breeze touched my face, and my skin crawled with fright.

This version of Eliphaz's experience describes a *light breeze* touching him, and his skin *crawling.* I believe that the Lord begins to visit us many times with a presence which, if we don't grieve Him, will culminate in some vision, revelation, or angelic visitation. But we have grieved Him many times. Fear and trembling, our hairs bristled, or something invisible crawling up our skin, has made us think, "This can't be God." Even when such kinds of manifestations have been less profound, we have grieved Him by scratching our skin, yawning, or turning over and going back to sleep.

The Lord once showed me a group of angels descending into a Christian lady's bedroom as she slept. Her spirit perceived their presence and dimly saw them, but she did not discern that they were good spirits, so she did not yield to the visitation. She became afraid and resisted them, and they left without delivering her blessing to her. Even in supernatural experiences, it is impossible to please God without faith, (Hebrews 11:6).

A great many kinds of voices, noises and presences can be disclosed to us—both good and evil ones—for a great many reasons. A sudden manifestation from the Lord may be clear and easy to discern, but if He comes slowly and gently, He's not so easy to discern sometimes. We need to remember that even if fear and goose-bumps result from a presence, that does not necessarily mean that it is not of God.

The natural flesh has been known to crawl with fright in the presence of God's holiness, and the natural mind has also been known to become troubled and go through changes at the visitation of a holy presence. Even Daniel, who had an excellent spirit, and was familiar with spiritual things and skillful in them, occasionally went through changes as a result of a supernatural manifestation.

Daniel 7:28 Hitherto is the end of the matter. As for me Daniel, my cogitations much troubled me, and my countenance changed in me: but I kept the matter in my heart.

Daniel 7:28 (amp) Here is the end of the matter. As for me, Daniel, my waking thoughts troubled and alarmed me much, and my cheerfulness of countenance was changed in me; but I kept the matter [of the interpreting angel's information] in my heart and mind.

Daniel 7:28 (tlb) That was the end of the dream. When I awoke, I was greatly disturbed, and my face was pale with fright, but I told no one what I had seen.

"My cogitations (thoughts) much troubled and alarmed me." "I was greatly disturbed." "My face was pale, with fright." This report of Daniel's is not a sweet and pleasant one. It is good and important to ask God to disclose supernaturals, and He will, but they won't always be pleasant. I have experienced hundreds of extraordinary manifestations of the Holy Spirit in my private time with Him, including audible voices, out-of-body experiences, visitations of angels, trances, and fire. Many of them have been quite sobering, for they occasionally arrested me, shook my body, contorted my face, controlled my tongue, and otherwise ordered me around.

Sometimes the way a manifestation comes means something. It may be an expression of the Spirit's mood at the time, and might symbolically speak to you. It's like a parabolic act or prophetic body language. If you can interpret it, that's fine. But if you don't understand it, and God doesn't explain it, then don't dwell on it too much. It may not be God's will for you to understand it then, or there may not be a special significance to it.

We must become knowledgeable about spiritual presences and sounds if we don't want to grieve God at His visitation. Many things, even answers to our prayers, have been hid from our eyes because we did not recognize the time of our visitation. Knowing only "the letter" of the Word of God, and not "the Spirit" of the Word, can make us think, "Fear has torment, so this fearful presence in my room cannot be of God. Jesus gives me perfect peace." But if we would be patient, slow to speak or jump to conclusions, a presence that visits us will eventually speak and make himself known, one way or the other, whether he is of God.

From my own experiences, I have found that when it was the Lord manifesting His presence somehow, as in a trance, I could draw myself away from that presence and get back into the natural realm if I wanted to. If I chose to, I could either yield fully to the anointing or resist it, and He would not insist on overwhelming me with His presence in order to force me to yield to Him.

On the other hand, when the devil shows up, he comes with a presence which insists on manifesting itself even though it is not welcome. He intimidates, threatens, and disturbs in such a way that it causes your spiritual armor to become activated almost automatically. When an invisible presence begins to draw near to you, and you want to know whether it is of God, just call upon the holy Blood of Jesus, mentally or vocally, and you'll find out.

When we become sensitive to presences coming around or upon us, we will find that they are not all from the Lord, and they are not all spiritual. My cat's presence on my bed once made me think it was God's presence. A small breeze might not be an angelic presence—it may be some air coming through the window. And some feelings on the flesh can be of demonic origin. However, many presences are from the Lord—even dark and disturbing ones

(Genesis 15:12; Daniel 4:19)—and they might disclose great revelations if we yield to them. God can make *darkness* His secret hiding place, (Psalms 18:11; 91:1); and a holy *fear* often precedes angelic visitations, (Luke 1:26).

In this study, we will examine several kinds of manifestations of spirits: how they sound, how they feel, what they might disclose as they present themselves, and certain conditions under which they may do so. Obviously, we cannot comment on all of the diverse kinds of spirits and their differences of administrations. But the few examined here may help us understand some basic principles and truths which will familiarize us with spiritual manifestations in a general way.

We must remember that many supernatural experiences come slowly and gradually, they begin with a simple, gentle presence. Therefore, it is important to be sensitive and know how to distinguish them when they come. Our degree of yieldedness, especially at the beginning, is, more often than not, the key factor which determines how much God can and will disclose when He visits us. His manifestation may depend on our faith. He will be disclosed unto us according to our faith, (Matthew 9:29).

Sometimes God imparts unto us the *gift of special faith* when He wants to disclose a special revelation. Our own faith may not be enough to help us apprehend what He would impart. Prophetic insights, confirmations of God's will, new anointings, and similar manifestations, are revelations from Above, and, may require faith from Above in order to be received.

The night season is the most likely and easiest time for us to perceive voices, noises, and presences. The neighborhood is quieter then, the physical body less active, and, particularly if you are alone, you are more able to mind spiritual things, if you would. "Be still and know that I am God."

When you are in prayer, you may ask God at what point you should end the prayer time. As an answer to you, He may "lift" His praying anointing off you when the praying time is over. Or He may leave it on you, and even increase it, when He wants you to stay in His presence longer because He has something special for you that night.

1Samuel 3:3-4 And ere the lamp of God went out in the temple of the Lord, where the Ark of God was, and Samuel was laid down to sleep; That the Lord called Samuel: and he answered, Here am I.

Young Samuel had completed his Temple-duties for the day. Before going to sleep, he read some Scriptures and prayed to the Lord. It was night-time. Eli, the Priest, was already in his own room sleeping, and the Temple echoed of silence. As Samuel was lying down, he heard the *audible voice* of the Lord. It may have come from inside the Ark of the Covenant, which was then resting in the Most Holy Place in that Temple.

Samuel was half-awake and half-asleep. The voice he heard was so real, so clear, that he answered back, "Here I am." He thought it was Eli and ran to him, not because it sounded like him, but because it was just as audible as a human voice. After he realized that it was the Lord calling him, he remained yielded to that supernatural voice and received the full message God came to disclose to him. I think that his right standing with God gave him faith and confidence to yield to His voice.

In contrast, King Nebuchadnezzar, after he had received the *word of the Lord* in a dream, and understood its interpretation by the help of the Prophet Daniel, did not take heed to that word of warning. A year later, consequently, an *audible voice* from Heaven "fell" on him, and his intellectual capacity was removed, (Daniel 4). He may or may not have felt it physically, but the anointing on that voice, within the hour, produced physical manifestations.

Daniel 4:28-33 All this came upon the king Nebuchadnezzar. At the end of twelve months he walked in the palace of the kingdom of Babylon. The

king spake, and said, Is not this great Babylon, that I have built for the house of the kingdom by the might of my power, and for the honour of my majesty? While the word was in the king's mouth, there fell a voice from heaven, saying, O king Nebuchadnezzar, to thee it is spoken; The kingdom is departed from thee. And they shall drive thee from men, and thy dwelling shall be with the beasts of the field: they shall make thee to eat grass as oxen, and seven times shall pass over thee, until thou know that the Most High ruleth in the kingdom of men, and giveth it to whomsoever He will. The same hour was the thing fulfilled upon Nebuchadnezzar: and he was driven from men, and did eat grass as oxen, and his body was wet with the dew of heaven, till his hairs were grown like eagles' feathers, and his nails like birds' claws.

Nebuchadnezzar suffered God's wrath because he prepared not his heart to seek the Lord when given a year to do so. He was abased by the voice from Heaven. Samuel, who had prepared himself in the things of God, was promoted as Prophet by the voice from the Lord. Our works, our words, and, most importantly, the motives, intentions, and attitudes of our hearts, largely determine what God will say to us at His visitation, how He will say it, and how His words will come to pass.

The Lord does not always speak when He visits us. He may allow us to feel His presence in some way without speaking or showing us anything. When times of refreshing come from the presence of the Lord, we might sense *rains* of the Spirit falling, *ointment* of the Spirit flowing, or *waves* of His glory flowing. Or we may feel *cool winds* of the Spirit blowing, the fluttering of angels' *wings,* or a *rushing mighty wind.* At angelic visitations, I have felt *cold chills* rushing up and down my body.

When the Holy Spirit discloses the fire anointing to purify, heal, or endow us, we may feel waves of *liquid fire* rolling up and down our bodies, *hot flames* resting upon us, or *flashes of light* burning around us.

Acts 2:1-4 And when the day of Pentecost was fully come, they were all with one accord in one place. And suddenly there came a sound from Heaven as of a rushing mighty wind, and it filled all the house where they were sitting. And there appeared unto them cloven tongues like as of fire, and it sat upon each of them. And they were all filled with the Holy Ghost, and began to speak with other tongues, as the Spirit gave them utterance.

Here, the 120 disciples first *heard* a sound from Heaven, then *saw* the cloven tongues of fire, and then *felt* that fire as it descended and sat upon each one of them. As a result, they were all filled with the power of the Holy Ghost, spoke in divine tongues, threw open the prayer room doors, and broke forth preaching the Gospel! You know they felt something!

After the Lord Jesus had been crucified, these brethren secluded themselves in the Upper Room for fear of the Pharisees. So the risen Jesus appeared unto them and encouraged them to expect and prepare for days of power. On the Day of Pentecost, the overwhelming presence of God emboldened them and made them drunk with the Spirit. He first came upon their flesh, then poured signs and wonders around and out of them. What we cannot do in the natural, the supernatural Spirit of God enables us when He shows up.

Jeremiah 20:9 (tev) But when I say, "I will forget the Lord and no longer speak in His Name," then Your message is like a burning fire deep within me. I try my best to hold it in, but can no longer keep it back.

Jeremiah's bones burned deep within him. The prophetic word of the Lord in him was "a *burning fire* shut up in my bones," (King James Version). He physically felt the fire of the Holy Ghost trying to flow through him. He tried his best to hold it in, but could no longer keep it back. He became weary and could not contain it. He probably experienced shakings and quakings in the spirit. Like the disciples, he had been anointed for a work which would not be restrained.

"The spirit of the prophet is subject to the prophet" (1Corinthians 14:32), but the divine Spirit of prophecy isn't! (A person can control his own spirit, but not God's.) Contrary to popular belief, there are some special times when a person simply must prophesy, and cannot hold it in. It may be the exception and not the rule but God has been known to arrest and entrance physical bodies and order demonstrations of His Spirit supernaturally.

Such kinds of manifestations of the Holy Ghost upon flesh can occur in public, and may involve a collective group of people. They can also occur in private, and often involve only a specified part of the body. On an earlier occasion, the Lord had touched Jeremiah's *mouth,* (Jeremiah 1:9).

The kind of presence visiting us, and its purpose, can be understood by the response it prompts, by the way it causes us to act, and by what results from it. You shall know it by its fruit, (Matthew 12:33). Jeremiah became anointed to *prophesy* after God had touched his *mouth.*

When a special presence from God comes upon or near you with no specific message, it may be appropriate to translate into words the sense of the presence that you're perceiving of Him. Then you'll know why He's there. Let's say, for example, that while you are in prayer in the presence of the Lord, you feel your hands being anointed with oil. The Lord may or may not speak words to explain that to you, but you can interpret His presence to mean that He wants to use your hands in His service somehow. And if you press into the realm of the spirit more deeply, you may find out exactly how He wants to use your hands.

That kind of situation is very similar to the operation of the gift of the word of knowledge, (1Corinthians 12:8). When this gift is in operation, the person may perceive an impression, and he can translate that impression into words by speaking what he feels and declaring what it means to him. For example, when God gives you *a word* about a sick woman because he wants to heal her, you may feel sick for a moment in the exact area of the body where she is sick. You may even feel as though you are a woman (even if you're not) in that same area, just until you've prayed for her.

The feelings, senses, and presences we perceive in the realm of the spirit, can, more often than not, be understood by the thoughts and feelings they inspire. It is because of this that Jesus does not always speak to us in order to explain His visions, visitations, and presences. And it is because of this that our input—our knowledge, understanding, personality, and ways of thinking—can occasionally help us interpret supernatural manifestations.

Chapter 2

PECULIAR DISCLOSINGS

Acts 17:27-28a (tev) He did this so that they would look for Him, and perhaps find Him as they felt around for Him. Yet God is actually not far from any one of us; as someone has said, "In Him we live and move and exist."

"For in Him we live and move and are!" (tlb). Jesus said, "Seek, and you shall find" (Matthew 7:7), when talking about the Holy Spirit. And Paul said that we can find God as we "feel around" for Him. Anything we separate unto the Lord, He sanctifies. When we present our bodies as a living sacrifice unto God, He makes us fit for His use and prepared for any kind of visitation of His Spirit, (Romans 12:1; 2Timothy 2:21). Then when He pours out of His Spirit upon our *flesh* (Acts 2:17), we can *feel* Him.

Now we should not go around seeking sensations, feelings, vibrations, or voices, in an attempt to experience something supernatural. In and by themselves, these things are fickle, pointless, and cannot be trusted. We should regard them only when they accompany, result from, or precede, a revelation from the Lord. We should also realize that they might not accompany, result from, or precede, a revelation from the Lord. Many supernatural experiences can occur without our perceiving them in a physical way.

The Patriarch Moses did not realize that his face was shining with the supernatural light of God. During his supernatural fast on Mount Sinai for forty days and forty nights, he had been gradually acclimated to the glory of God without realizing it:

Exodus 34:29 And it came to pass, when Moses came down from Mount Sinai with the two tables of testimony in Moses' hand, when he came down from the mount, that Moses wist not that the skin of his face shone while he talked with Him.

The Apostle Peter did not know he was being translated out of prison supernaturally by the angel of the Lord until after it happened. While it was occurring, he knew not that it was true, but thought he saw a vision:

Acts 12:9 And he went out, and followed him; and wist not that it was true which was done by the angel; but thought he saw a vision.

The Nazarite, Samson, did not know that God had removed His anointing from him until he got into a fight and lost. In his pride, he thought that he could simply go out as at other times and abuse the anointing of God on him:

Judges 16:20 And she said, The Philistines be upon thee, Samson. And he awoke out of sleep, and said, I will go out as at other times before, and shake myself. And he wist not that the Lord was departed from him.

Many people are healed, blessed, and anointed in Church services, or in private prayer, and do not know it when it happened. As Christians lay anointed hands on people and pray for them, they often do not feel anything going through them, yet many things result from those prayers. And God often guides our lives in answer to prayer without necessarily speaking distinctly. His providence alone can speak.

When we do feel something as the Holy Spirit works through us, it is either because God wants us to perceive it for some reason, or because we are sensitive and can easily pick up spiritual activity around us. Praying and living in the spirit by faith makes it easy to perceive activity in that realm by faith.

A person can become so sensitive to spiritual things that he can hear voices and other sounds even when God is not directly initiating them. I have heard people's voices sometimes so much so that I had to bind them in the Name of Jesus. Some spiritual voices, noises, presences, and sights, are directly inspired by the Lord, but many times they may be perceived as we simply go about our natural activities. One may or may not benefit from what he perceives, and can choose to close those openings in the spiritual realm by the authority he has in the Name of Jesus. From time to time, I have had to do just that.

Ecclesiastes 10:20 Curse not the king, no not in thy thought; and curse not the rich in their bedchamber: for a bird of the air shall carry the

UNDERSTANDING VOICES, NOISES & PRESENCES IN THE SPIRITUAL REALM

voice, and that which hath wings shall tell the matter.

That which "hath wings" can be an angel. God makes His angels into *spirits* or *winds* (Hebrew: *ruwach;* Psalms 104:4), and as they fly to and fro throughout the earth they can carry messages. If people are talking about you behind your back, you might hear them in the realm of the spirit, because the winged messengers can carry voices which may tell you some things.

A *voice carrier* may be your own angel which is looking out for you, or someone else's; he may be sent from the Third Heaven, or he may be stationed in your own neighborhood. Instead of an angel, he may be a human spirit flying by, or he may be an evil *wind.* There are, it may be, so many kinds of *winds in the air.*

In several out-of-body experiences which I have had, I came into the presence of people. At times, I flew by them, at times walked by them, and at times stood by them. At times, I could hear their thoughts, and at times spoke to them. At times, I could tell that they knew there was an invisible presence there (me), and that they could faintly hear my voice. Perhaps some thoughts, sounds, and presences we perceive, are those of our brethren who are *with us in the spirit.*

Colossians 2:5 For though I be absent in the flesh, yet am I with you in the spirit, joying and beholding your order, and the stedfastness of your faith in Christ.

Here, the Apostle Paul says, "I am with you in the spirit." He suggests that he was able to see what the Christians at Colosse were doing, discern the stedfastness of their faith in the Lord, and rejoice in their midst right along with them. In his letter to the Romans, Paul wrote, "Rejoice with them that do rejoice, and weep with them that weep," (Romans 12:15). Paul knew some things about intercessory prayer and being *touched* with the *feeling* of another person's infirmities (Hebrews 4:15), because he knew how to be *with them* in the spirit.

I occasionally hear voices when I am involved in spiritual things or in natural things. Besides hearing the voices of Jesus, the Holy Spirit, and angels, I have heard those of people, many of whom I know personally. They would either speak to each other about me, or directly to me; would speak few words, or many; would bless, or disturb me; would speak truths, or lies. Sometimes I could tell that they were actually speaking those words in reality; at times, I knew they were only thinking those things (though they themselves may not even realize it).

My own conscience, subconscious thinking, and born-again spirit, can also speak loudly unto me. All of a sudden, while I'm going about my normal daily business, I may hear a statement made, a word, a voice of some kind saying something to me. As I pay attention to that voice, and think on what was said, I may find that it was actually my own spirit speaking up so I could consciously apprehend ("get") what he's saying. This is one way that I preach to myself. Some of the points I make in my books, even whole paragraphs, have come about this way, but very rarely.

I have heard several musicians testify that they would "hear" musical notes or songs and translate them into the natural realm. One musician, the late Miles Davis, also said he "saw" colors and was able to translate them on his trumpet. In my own experience, some of my writings have come via simple thoughts, impressions and ideas, via words, sentences and phrases, and occasionally via supernatural visions and dreams. Although these may be biblically-based (because my mind is renewed to the Word of God; Romans 12:2), I verify and enlarge upon them through further biblical study. I have also thought that maybe some of the numbers I have seen in the spirit represent the numerical value of the revelation knowledge given me by the Spirit.

My born-again Holy Spirit-led spirit knows what's good for me because he's closer to Jesus than my natural mind is. But his voices (my spirit's varied[1] voices, tones, and moods) challenge me many times because they often jar my natural way of thinking. Though he speaks only what the Word of God says, he does so in an extraordinary and colorful array of idioms, puns, parables, symbols, and witty phrases which, if I didn't know the Bible and the Holy Spirit's personality, would make me doubt whether I'm really being spiritually-minded. My spirit is always trying to get me to follow him as he follows the Lord, but he often does so in interesting and challenging ways which really require faith.

Many *voices* and other spiritual manifestations are nothing more than products of our emotions and imaginations. These also need to be checked according to the Bible. Only the Word of God is able to make an accurate distinction between natural-mindedness (thoughts inspired by one's own ways of thinking, even though they may be good), and spiritual-mindedness (thoughts inspired by one's own Holy Spirit-led spirit). Only the Word of God can draw the line between a person's mind and his spirit, (Hebrews 4:12).

Now if I find that the voices I hear are only in my imagination, and that they don't edify, teach, encourage, or inspire me in my walk with God, I can lay my hands on my head and take authority over those thoughts and bring them under the control of the Holy Spirit, in the Name of Jesus:

2Corinthians 10:4-5 (For the weapons of our warfare are not carnal, but mighty through God to the pulling down of strongholds;) Casting down imaginations, and every high thing that exalteth itself against the knowledge of God, and bringing into captivity every thought to the obedience of Christ.

The Bible says that to be naturally-minded is death, but to be spiritually-minded is life and peace, (Romans 8:5). Without the devil himself actually being present in a direct way, the natural mind tends to think negatively and entertain vain imaginations. It may also want to speak by a distinct voice. Hence the need to cast down those imaginations and bring every thought (and thought patterns, "strongholds") to the obedience of Christ.

If such voices are actually of demonic spirits, then, too, I resist them in the Name of Jesus, claiming the power in the Blood of Jesus against them, and they flee:

James 4:7 Submit yourselves therefore to God. Resist the devil, and he will flee from you.

When they are in fact voices that I can pick up on my "spiritual antenna," I can choose to go on listening, or to turn off that "spiritual radio." So I ask the Lord. If it is His doing, I go on listening. If not, I can bind them in the Name of Jesus, (Matthew 18:18). When He turns on the "radio," I listen; when it goes on "by itself," I can choose whether or not to listen.

Ever since the electric radio transmitter was invented, innumerable programs, along with the spiritual presences they project, have increasingly been sent out into the atmosphere. These presences can greatly influence lives in a positive or negative way. The wise King Solomon wrote that a dream can come as a result of much business and activity, (Ecclesiastes 5:3a).

This shows us that dreams, visions, thoughts, impressions, feelings, vibrations, and presences—all of which can influence and guide a person's life—can result from sound activity in the local airwaves which are being transmitted electrically. In a spiritual parallel, Joel prophesied that divinely suggested dreams, visions, audible voices, spiritual presences, and other supernatural manifestations will be perceived as a result of divinely suggested words and activity in the air when God sends an outpouring of His Holy Spirit,

(Acts 2:17-21).

Christians and non-Christians alike can perceive spiritual or natural activity in the air. Normally, a radio receiver is used to hear radio programs, but there are a few cases of people with extremely sensitive ears who occasionally hear radio transmissions without a radio receiver. Some hear only vague transmissions with static, some hear clearly; some hear them very rarely, and some can hear them almost "at will."

The explanation for these cases is either that these people are predisposed to spiritual sensitivity from the time of their birth, or that they have practiced some form of ungodly religious exercises and entered a mystical realm, or that God has enabled them to see and hear in the realm of the spirit for His glory, such as for a prophetic prayer ministry.

Jeremiah 10:22 (niv) Listen! The report is coming—a great commotion from the land of the north! It will make the towns of Judah desolate, a haunt of jackals.

"Listen! There is a sound of a commotion, a declaration of war against us!" While he was in the spirit, the Prophet Jeremiah heard this news report, knew where it came from, and understood what it entailed.

At the time of the Persian Gulf crisis in 1991, on the eve of the United Nations' attack on Saddam Hussain's forces in Kuwait, I had a supernatural *panoramic vision.* (For a more detailed description and study of this kind of vision, including eleven other kinds which I specifically identify and define, please refer to my book, *Understanding Supernatural Visions According to the Bible*). In the spirit, I *audibly* heard millions of Americans all across the United States rejoicing and celebrating, and *visually* saw them jumping and dancing in the streets in many ticker-tape parades. This revelation lasted about 5 seconds, but I can't really be sure because time, as it is understood in the natural realm, can't be measured in the spiritual realm.

I could only conclude from this vision that the war which would begin the next day was not going to occur, hence the celebrations. I thought that there would be no war, or, at the most, a very short battle with a minimum of casualties. When I watched television the next night and saw a spectacular display of air-land warfare, I questioned not my revelation, but its proper interpretation.

However, after a few short months of war, with a minimum of casualties on the side of the U.N. forces, it is understandable that Americans would rejoice the way that we did—in reality, and in my prophetic vision. The celebrations of victory which I saw on television during the summer of 1991 were briefly captured in my supernatural vision five months earlier.

In addition, I had had three relevant dreams from the Lord prior to this war. Each of them suggested that Saddam Hussain would be confronted militarily, and that he would back off grinning and showing empty hands.

As recent history confirms, that's exactly what happened. Saddam and all his armed forces were powerless (they had "empty hands") against the United Nations, and they backed off in that they quickly released their hostages, and many thousands of their own soldiers gladly surrendered.

Other servants and handmaids of God received visions about the war in the Gulf too, and they were confirmed as they also came to pass.

In 2005 and again in 2007, I saw heavenly visions revealing the heavenly design in the Iraq war. The stars in the Star-Spangled Banner joined with the stars in the sky and danced in a marvelous formation as U.S. fighter jets flew across the sky over America and headed over the Atlantic to go fight. The event has eternal ramifications and is more spiritual than most can fathom.

Amos 3:7 Surely the Lord God will do nothing, but He revealeth His secret unto His servants the prophets.

Endnotes

[1]   Our spiritual eyes may occasionally "see our teachers" (those who have instructed us in the things of life, and in the Word of God) leading us by the way which we should go. Our spiritual ears may also "hear a word" *behind us* (in the back of our minds, just behind our conscious awareness) advising us in our decisions throughout life. These varied visions and voices can be supernatural apparitions and audible voices. But, more often than not, they are simply our own spirits counseling our minds with the wisdoms we have received and stored in a corner of our subconscious for just when we will need them, even though they may occasionally appear and sound like our former teachers and mentors. And the more adversity and affliction we may experience in life, the more will we need, and summon, those wisdoms, (Isaiah 30:20-21).

Chapter 3

ANGELIC INVOLVEMENT

2Kings 6:8-12 (amp) When the king of Syria was warring against Israel, counseling with his servants he said, In such and such a place shall be my camp. Then the man of God sent to the king of Israel, saying, Beware that you pass not such a place; for the Syrians are coming down there. Then the king of Israel sent to the place of which [Elisha] told and warned him, and thus protected and saved himself there repeatedly. Therefore the mind of the king of Syria was greatly troubled by this thing. He called his servants and said, Will you show me who of us is for

the king of Israel? One of his servants said, None, my lord, O king; but Elisha, the prophet who is in Israel, tells the king of Israel the words that you speak in your bedchamber.

Repeatedly, over and over again, the king of Israel knew his enemy's battle-strategies because his friend, the Prophet Elisha, could hear in the realm of the spirit. Time and time again, he heard what the Syrians were planning and warned his king faithfully. I'm sure he also saw some things as his spirit would occasionally enter the enemy's camp and spy on them. And not only did he see the enemy, but he also saw the angels of God which ministered to him:

2Kings 6:16-17 (amp) Elisha answered, Fear not; for those with us are more than those with them. Then Elisha prayed, Lord, I pray You, open his eyes that he may see. And the Lord opened the young man's eyes, and he saw; and behold, the mountain was full of horses and chariots of fire round about Elisha.

Elisha prayed "for his servant's eyes to be opened" so that he would be able to see the angels. If he himself saw those angels too, it was because he was walking in the supernatural naturally. He did not necessarily pray for his own eyes to be opened on that occasion because they had already been opened and enabled to see—first by his association with and learning from the Prophet Elijah (2Kings 2:15), and finally by receiving his prophetic mantle. Therefore, he was able to penetrate his prophetic "eagle's eyes" into the spiritual realm and see into it, at times, by his own volition.

Further, Elisha did not repeatedly ask the Lord to open his ears each time he heard the Syrians in the spiritual realm because they, too, had already been opened and anointed to discern spiritual activity—again, at times, by an act of his own volition. Depending upon the type of anointing in our lives, and upon our knowledge, our faith, and our motives, we can enjoy a corresponding degree of liberty in spiritual things. The gifts of the Holy Spirit are *given us* (1Corinthians 12:7-11) so that we can indeed be laborers *together* with God, (1Corinthians 3:9).

The President of the United States of America needs some friends like Elisha. As a leader of a great nation, he himself can receive some insights from the Lord on how to lead—even supernaturally. But he is not anointed to see and hear spiritual things as clearly or frequently as God's prophets. Even his very best advisors are limited. As a rule, they base their wisdom on their own logical deductions, not on spiritual insights from the Lord; albeit God uses events in providence to bring about His designs in the affairs of earth.

As King David was surrounded by the choicest military men of his day, Elisha was surrounded by the best soldiers from God's angelic army. His servant was surrounded by them only when he was near Elisha. When King Jehoram welcomed Elisha's ministry, he became surrounded by those angels, too. Of course, outside of Elisha's presence, those men still had their own unique anointings and their own angels around them serving them.

A friend of mine preached the Word of God one night and afterward ministered in the gifts of the Spirit. When he was done, the pastor of the church asked me to say a few words to the congregation and, as I did, I started ministering to the people with the same kinds of gifts my friend just had, to those he had not prayed for. I believe the anointing on him, and the angels around him, affected me as I came inside their circle, and enhanced the manifestation of the Holy Spirit in that church that night.

Our proximity to a special anointing of the Lord and to His special angels can, with or without our conscious awareness, influence us—our behavior, our lives, our ministries. Remember how King Saul was turned into *another man* and prophesied with Samuel's company of prophets while he was in their presence? (1Samuel 10:5-6).

Aimee Semple McPherson, who lived a century ago, was a mighty woman of God with a special anointing of the Holy Spirit upon her and angels ministering for her. When the great Evangelist Smith Wigglesworth preached in her church in Los Angeles, California, his own anointing increased and manifested more greatly than in any other place he had ever preached before, according to his own testimony. When the troops of God get together, their power multiplies! (Leviticus 26:8).

Those who welcome God's anointed servants come into the presence of distinguished angels, authorities, and powers. Oftentimes we can perceive peculiar anointings on God's servants, but we may also sense angelic presences. When we yield to them, those persons and their angels may disclose some things to us in some way. It's like when someone has a special healing gift upon them—if you acknowledge and receive it, you can be healed by it.

The *prophetic word of the Lord* which came to the prophets of God in the Bible did not always come by visions. Prophecies occasionally came as words, and were delivered by angels. They may have spoken in the first person ("I am the Lord..."), but angels were the vessels sent to voice His words. Even when the Heavenly Father spoke audibly at Jesus' baptism, and again at His transfiguration, His voice was disclosed through the ministry of angels. Without them intermediating, the voice of the Almighty would consume the whole creation. The angels assisted in the creation of all things, even though the Bible says, "God said... God made," and they are still ministering for us together with God.

As angels can reveal God's voice unto us, they can also reveal other sounds from Him. When the Syrians besieged and threatened the city of Samaria in the time of Elisha, the Lord made the Syrian army to hear a noise of chariots and horses, the noise of a great army, (2Kings 7:5-7). The Syrians fled at this fearful sound, and thus Samaria was saved. Perhaps the same angels which served Israel during King David's reign were involved here, and operated in much the same way:

2Samuel 5:24 And let it be, when thou hearest the sound of a going in the tops of the mulberry trees, that then thou shalt bestir thyself: for then shall the Lord go out before thee, to smite the host of the Philistines.

When the Lord is going before us in some project, He might bestir us by the *sound* of "a going," (that is, "a walking or marching"). Or He might bestir us by the *feeling* of a going. Or He might simply *say,* "Go."

Spiritual presences can usually be interpreted very much as natural presences are interpreted. The fire of God can purify us spiritually the way that natural fire can purify silver and gold, therefore, a manifestation of fire may mean that God is purifying us. In the same way, the kinds of sounds we hear in the spiritual realm can usually be interpreted the way natural sounds are interpreted. I have heard *doors close* in the spirit, and knew that God was closing the door on an opportunity that came my way. We can ask God to open a particular door for us, but the Spirit may say, "No," as He said to Paul, (Acts 16:6-7).

Chapter 4

SPIRITUAL PRESENCES AROUND PEOPLE

1Corinthians 12:1 (amp)   Now about the spiritual gifts (the special endowments of supernatural energy), brethren, I do not want you to be misinformed.

Now concerning supernatural manifestations of special gifts, endowments, and "energies" through people, brethren, God does not want us to be ignorant (without knowledge) or misinformed (with wrong knowledge). We know that the gifts of the Spirit are given *to* this Christian, and *to* that one, and that they operate *through* them. Yet the gifts are not the only things that can manifest through God's people. As we stand before an anointed Christian, we may feel, hear, or see, any of a great variety of spiritual activities around him. A *supernatural energy* of some sort with which a servant of God has been especially endowed, can almost automatically—without being directly revealed by God—be perceived by a spiritually sensitive person near him.

In the presence of a psalmist, we might hear music and songs "coming out of him" (in a sense) though he may not be singing or playing an instrument at that time. A soldier may present invisible battles around him which may be perceived by the people in his presence. A pastor may present love, a writer may present books, and a preacher may be preaching in the spirit while silent in the natural. An intercessor may be praying, in the spirit, while socializing or going about his normal daily business.

At this writing, I am aware that someone in particular (who is also a writer) is praying for God to lead me in the writing of this book. I think it's more than just my imagination: that person is *with me in the spirit.*

You see, the human spirit, the "inner man of the heart," is occupied in eternal things even when the physical body is not. He can also extend himself beyond the limitations of the body and perform extraordinary tasks, and he may not even realize it when it is happening. When his spirit is active this way, those who are spiritually sensitive may perceive his presence.

When we constantly feel as though someone is near us, or we feel an urgency to talk with them when there is no apparent reason to, it is usually due to an inner witness or spiritual prompting *in us.* But it can also be that their presence is *with us* to some extent. Just as an *audible voice* can be heard by the *spiritual ears* or the *physical ears,* so likewise a *spiritual presence* can be perceived by the *spiritual body* or the *physical body.*

The people who are especially close to us in some way, such as our loved ones, are generally with us in a general way. They are in our prayers, and we are in their prayers, so we are especially connected and easily within reach of each other. But those relationships largely involve emotional feelings, and not always spiritual feelings or presences. When there is a disclosing in the spiritual realm—either God Himself "turns on our radio receiver," or our sensitive "antenna" pick up a reception freely—then we might really perceive some spiritual presences.

Such a presence may be that of someone we know and recognize, or of a stranger whom the Lord is presenting to us. In intercession, occasionally we can literally feel upon our flesh the person's weakness that the Lord wants us to pray about, and we may not even know who the person is:

Hebrews 4:15a For we have not an High Priest which cannot be touched with the feeling of our infirmities.

As Jesus in Heaven intercedes for us, He is easily *touched* with the *feeling* of our infirmities: He easily feels what we are going through. He is our High Priest, and He eternally intercedes before the Heavenly Father on our behalf, (Hebrews 7:25). As we intercede in prayer for others, we, too, can feel their infirmities in such a way that we know we are "with them" in the spirit helping to lighten their load, minister their healing, bring about their deliverance, and order their paths aright. Our very senses (touch, sight, smell, taste and hearing) can become so trained at discerning presences that they will easily perceive spirits and quickly identify them, (Hebrews 5:14). The vibrations ("vibes") you get when you come near a certain person, or a certain place, or a certain thing, may indicate a particular kind of presence—good or evil—in or around or otherwise involved with them.

Admittedly, it takes faith to yield to these things, and when we do we will find that they are not all experiences from the Holy Spirit. And when they are inspired of Him, they are not always going to be pleasant experiences. However, the Lord promises to give us spiritual discernment in these areas, and promises that great signs and wonders will result for His glory.

Are we able to feel the presence of someone who has died? Only in our imaginations, and our thoughts of them can affect our emotions, which in turn can affect our physical sensibilities. If we don't know how to distinguish between our *inward* experiences and our *outward* ones, we might believe that a dead person is with us supernaturally simply because we had some kind of thought or impression about them. Our thoughts, visions and dreams of them—along with the physical/emotional feelings they may cause—are, for the most part, inward (mental) ideas of our own making.

Some supernatural experiences which are indeed outward, and not of our own making, may symbolically involve a person who is dead. When a Christian dies and goes to Heaven, he is not normally informed in detail of earthly affairs and he does not participate in them in a physical way. He is kept informed about earthly matters only in a general way, if at all, and is only permitted to influence them through his prayers. (The Christians in Heaven are praying for us; Revelation 8:4). On those occasions when he is so permitted, we might think we sense his presence around us in some way. But, as with heavenly voices, such a presence (if it is more than imaginary) can only be a symbolic representation of him, presented by the ministry of the angels. It cannot be that person's literal presence visiting us from Heaven because God does not permit actual appearances by, or communication with, departed spirits, (Deuteronomy 18:9-14).

A person who is grieving over the death of a loved one would like to be comforted by his presence. But since the dead person is actually in another world now, only an angel can minister that comfort, and only as the Lord leads him to. However, most presences of this kind are nothing more than our emotions. The fact that we can so quickly and easily "invoke" a dead person's presence by simply cherishing and adoring a memento of him proves that his "presence" begins and ends with our emotions and, therefore, disqualifies it as being supernatural.[1] Only when there is a specific purpose in it, God may allow us to perceive a heavenly visitor in some way. And that visitor can only be *the angel of that person's presence,* and not that person's actual presence.

Paul knew some things about heavenly goings-on. He tells us that we are "compassed about with a great cloud of witnesses, the spirits of just men made perfect," (Hebrews 12:1, 23). What did he mean? Did he mean that the saints of God who have died and gone to Heaven can return to us and compass us about? No. Those spirits cannot personally communicate and present themselves to us. He meant that when Christians die and go to Heaven[2] they are made perfect (sinless) and, together with Jesus, they pray for us who are still on earth, (Hebrews 7:25; Revelation 8:4). He also meant to say that they surround the saints on earth insofar as they are in accord with us and occupied in the same business of the Kingdom of God as we are. The whole family of saints, both in Heaven and earth, is named after Jesus, and we are all, as a holy Temple, *fitly framed together* for a habitation of God *through the Spirit,* (Ephesians 2:21-22; 3:15).

When Jesus was transfigured (temporarily changed) before His disciples (Luke 9:28-35), and Moses and Elijah appeared in glory (splendor) and spoke of His decease which He should accomplish at Jerusalem, the Lord's own surrounding *aura,* as it shone through Him, visibly displayed the prophets that were with Him. Within the confines of that aura, they were able to *appear* and *speak.* They didn't descend[3] from Heaven, as did Jesus after His resurrection, but were able to "show up" in and with Jesus insofar as He had embraced and exemplified their ministries. *"In Him* give all the prophets witness," (Acts

10:43). If the aura of His immediate presence had begun to shine more brightly, some of the other prophets would also have begun to show up in it. Moses and Elijah appeared first because they, respectively, represented the Law of God and all His prophets.

This can occur in our lives also. Within the confines of our own surrounding aura, there are people, places, things, and spirits which we've embraced and allowed to become a part of us. If God shines His light on our aura, those people, places, things, and spirits, will begin to become seeable, with the most prominent ones showing up first. The dynamic of "influence (or, impartation) by association" operates here. Invisible things in one's life can influence another person who spends time in his presence; hence, Solomon's advice to choose your friends and teachers wisely, (Proverbs 13:20).

A person's spouse, family members, and friends, (those which are alive), are key parts of his life, so they are the easiest to sense around him. So are his occupation, talents, and inclinations. When people come near him, some of those things may begin to *appear* and *speak*. It is then that a person with discernment can, possibly, see who he is talking with, whether or not he is really of God, what are the main things that have surrounded and influenced his life in the past, and what is going on in his life presently.

Portions of a person's future might also be seen around him, if the Holy Spirit permits (1Corinthians 12:7), but they are more difficult to see. The future is less often revealed than the past or present because it isn't completely predetermined and unchangeable, and also because it may not be to anyone's advantage to know it.

Some Christian churches have a tradition of painting the departed saints with a halo or aura, and with certain specific items within that aura. By examining the items depicted in a saint's aura, we can know what his life represented, what he embraced and agreed with, and what kind of anointing he operated in. Many paintings of Christ show an image of a *dove* (the biblical symbol of the

Holy Spirit as pure and *harmless;* Matthew 10:16) descending or resting directly over His head. And many paintings of the disciples in the Upper Room on the Day of Pentecost show an image of *flames of fire* (the biblical symbol of the Holy Spirit as *dynamic power;* Acts 1:8) descending or resting directly over their heads.

That these kinds of spiritual presences around people are real, and that they do indeed show up in them now and then, is further evidenced by the fact that it is usually much easier to pray and minister to a person when they are right there in your presence. When I get visions of people who are not immediately around me, they are limited to a certain class of revelations. But when people stand before me, I may also perceive some presences around them, which provides for me an added dimension, and can also help me to respond with the appropriate *word of the Lord* for them.

I have rarely had visions or revelations of saints who have gone to Heaven, but they can occur. Supernaturally, the angels of God may communicate to us in a vision involving the people in Heaven. Angels which once ministered for the saints in Heaven can also minister unto us who are still on earth, at times in similar ways.

Angelic fellow-servants of the prophets and saints which have lived and died before us are still ministering for the saints on earth, (Revelation 19:10; 22:9). Therefore, those angels may occasionally reveal a bit of the knowledge or character of the persons they have ministered for in the past, and speak to us in their stead. I believe this explains the validity of the supernatural voices and visions received by the great St. Joan of Arc, and others like her, who heard audible voices and received messages "from the saints" in Heaven which were confirmed to be of God.

God's angels have a mediatory ministry between Heaven and earth. Any God-inspired vision or dream of a person who has died and gone to Heaven can only be a visual one, ministered by the angel of that person's presence on earth. Such a vision cannot be an *apparition,* which is an *actual appearing.* Any voice, sound, or presence, claiming to be that of a person who has died, can only be a manifestation of a deceiving spirit. God would not have us to be ignorant about all these things because He doesn't want us to be deceived. That's why He condemns spiritualist mediums, people who claim to invoke the spirits of the dead and communicate with them, (Deuteronomy 18:9-14).

At a funeral, a man's family and friends may be mourning his death, and may not even be sure if he made it to Heaven. If he did, the further he enters in through the gates of that City, the less will he think of earthly things. In that very day, his natural concerns perish, (Psalms 146:4). But if God wants to minister comfort to those mourners, the angel of that man's presence may bring it. And if his family still *feels* his presence at home when he's no longer there, that *feeling* is either a residue of his soul temporarily lingering, an emotionally-incited imagination, or both. Good or bad things that may have been in his life largely make up that residue.

If a person died without having Jesus Christ in his life, and went to hell, feelings of him, or evil spirits which were in him, may disturb his loved ones. In that case, they should pray in the Name of Jesus and rebuke those spirits. By claiming the Blood of Jesus, praying in the Holy Ghost, reading the Word of God aloud, and anointing the home with oil, evil presences are dispelled.

Endnotes

1   There are also spiritual presences which manifest when spiritist mediums summon the spirits of the dead in séances, (Leviticus 19:31). But these are manifestations of evil spirits, (familiar spirits, demons) intending to deceive and defile gullible, uninformed people who would inquire into these forbidden areas.

2   It should be understood that not every person who dies goes to Heaven. The Bible clearly shows that sinners, those who do not believe on Christ and serve Him, go to hell torment when they die (Luke 16:19-31), and will be eternally cast into the Lake of Fire on the Great Judgment Day which is soon to come, (Revelation 20:15).

3   This showing up of Moses and Elijah with Jesus is often interpreted as a literal return from among the dead. However, the context shows they were simply "made seeable with open eyes" and they were clothed with "honor" (glory). Jesus was visibly changed (made to shine) in the sight of His disciples in order to show them that the glorious Law of God (Moses) and the Word of His prophets (Elijah) emanate from Jesus, speak of His death from the beginning, and will find their final glorification in His resurrection. Moses and Elijah literally appearing outside of Jesus' splendor-ful aura-circle, clothed with honor, would not have shown that.

The disciples, unable to understand this profound message because they were oppressed with sleep, needed to have these things disclosed to them for future reference, (Mark 9:9).

Chapter 5

SPIRITUAL PRESENCES IN CERTAIN PLACES

Exodus 25:8 And let them make me a sanctuary; that I may dwell among them.

There are many kinds of spiritual voices, noises and presences in this world, and many of them are housed in specific places. When God instructed Moses to build a sanctuary for Him, it was so that His presence may dwell there. A building, a house, a church, or a theater, can be indwelt with spirits (good or evil) which may manifest themselves occasionally and be perceived.

Other places as well can be dwellingplaces for spirit beings. Neighborhoods, cities, and whole nations, may have distinct principalities and powers hovering in high places over them, (Ephesians 6:12; Daniel 10:13).

In the beginning, the presence of God's Spirit moved upon the *face of the waters* and His voice spoke everything into existence and blessed it. But His presence especially rested on planet earth because man was placed *here,* (Genesis 1).

When Adam and Eve first sinned in the Garden of Eden, they heard the voice (or, sound) of the Lord God walking *in the Garden* in the cool of the day. Then they tried to hide themselves from the presence of the Lord. The Garden was peculiarly blessed because in it was the Tree of Life, and after Adam and Eve were cast out of it, angels of God with a sword of fire were stationed there to guard it, (Genesis 3).

The Tabernacle of Moses was also an especially anointed place, (Exodus 25:8). God dwelt among His people Israel, but His presence more especially manifested in the Tent of the Congregation, even more in the Holy Place, and most gloriously in the Holy of Holies. God had told Moses that *the Tabernacle* shall be sanctified by His glory. It was directly from the Ark of the Covenant, which lay in the Holy of Holies, that the Lord spoke audibly to the High Priest when he entered. This Most Holy Place of the Tabernacle was so especially anointed with God's presence that only the High Priest could enter it to speak with God—under the strictest of guidelines—and only once a year.

Some places are more anointed than others. We often think that our properties and possessions cannot be anointed with the Holy Spirit and are not served by angels. But they are. In the time of King David, the Ark of the Covenant physically contained a tangible presence which could kill (1Chronicles 13:7), and which could bless, (1Chronicles 13:14). Even in our present Age of Grace, there is significance to this. Consider Paul's *anointed prayer cloths:*

Acts 19:11-12 (amp) And God did unusual and extraordinary miracles by the hands of Paul, So that handkerchiefs or towels or aprons which had touched his skin were carried away and put upon the sick, and their diseases left them, and the evil spirits came out of them.

Now we do not want to worship our church buildings or their furniture, or our homes and personal belongings. They are all lifeless materials which serve us in the earth. But when they are committed unto the Lord and used in His service, as were Paul's handkerchiefs, He calls them His property and places His anointing on them. And His angels guard those properties.

A church building where Christians congregate to worship the Lord in spirit and in truth can house the *glory* (the *manifest presence* of the Lord). In the realm of the spirit, I have seen the *glory cloud* of God in some churches. I have also seen churches without it. Either a ministry has become backslidden and the glory has departed from it (1Samuel 4:22), or maybe that ministry was never blessed of the Lord to begin with.

Malachi 1:3 And I hated Esau, and laid his mountains and his heritage waste for the dragons of the wilderness.

When the Lord made Esau's estate (the land of Edom) desolate, it became inhabited by *dragons* (strange creatures). Deserted cities and places can become inhabited by spiritual dragons (demonic creatures) and are commonly called "ghost towns." That *spooky feeling* you may get in a ghost town may in fact be an actual *presence* there. The same is true of "haunted houses." Spiritual beings may reside in a house whether or not people are living there. The house itself does not haunt, but *a being* there does.

When I was a teenager, I began having some extraordinary nightmares in which demons would torment me. I was not a Christian at that time, so I felt helpless against those forces. I knew it wasn't simply my subconscious imagination disturbing me because those experiences were more than natural, and because they had also occurred while I was awake.

I came home from school one day and there was no one home, and everything seemed very quiet. It was then that I was able to perceive their spiritual presence and sounds. (When you are still, you can more easily perceive some things if they are there.) I did not know what to do, so I turned on the television, the radio, and put on some records, all at the same time, and very loud. I thought, if possible, that I would disturb them for a change, at least until I went to sleep. But it was only after I moved from that apartment that I was free from those spirits. This is why we should pray when moving into a new home.

Kenneth E. Hagin writes of visiting an old church building because it was a tourist attraction. The Lord had been trying to lead him not to go there, but he did not understand or follow that leading. While in that church building with his young son, Ken, Jr., a spirit came up through the floor and grabbed the boy, pulling him to the ground and stupefying him for a few minutes. The tour guide casually responded, "Don't worry. This happens all the time. He'll be alright in a little while." This happens all the time? It must be a resident spirit in that place!

Carnegie Hall, a famous palatial entertainment theater in New York City, houses a supernatural presence. Many famous entertainers from many parts of the world have entertained there and, perhaps without their knowledge, have transacted spiritual business. One famous entertainer, Liza Minelli, testified that she literally felt an awesome presence like an electrical shock come upon her when she first performed on the stage there. A famous musician, the late Leonard Bernstein, said that he was so overwhelmed by a powerful presence when he first performed there, that he could not remember even a moment of his performance. Another famous musician also confessed that "there are many voices, sounds and presences of people who have performed there over many decades still on that stage, and even within every nook and cranny of Carnegie Hall. And those voices and spiritual presences assist in the amplifying of the voices and music of those who perform there now."

I believe that those supernatural experiences could be the effect of the collective spirit of the audiences observing, applauding, and going out to the performers in the realm of the spirit. Yet, such presences have often been perceived at Carnegie Hall when no one was performing. The fact that the very walls seem to repeat back to an observer that which has been performed there, and that the stage seems to continue to vibrate with the *echoes* and *energies* of those who have played and danced there, indicates that there are invisible beings there. The same could be said of other theaters, clubs, stadiums, and other places where people have poured their "soul-energies" out of themselves in some way. Again, this is either because a residue of their soul may tend to linger after their departure, or because the spirits which operated in their lives remain there, or both.

The spirits in a liquor store or bar must be cast out when a minister of the Gospel buys that property to make a church out of it. Spiritual warfare often takes place when a Christian moves into a home which was previously indwelt by ungodly people, when he enters an unbeliever's home or business, or when he travels through certain cities or neighborhoods.

Ephesians 6:12 For we wrestle not against flesh and blood, but against principalities, against powers, against the rulers of the darkness of this world, against spiritual wickedness in high places.

The enemies being rebuked in prayer-battles are not of flesh and blood (humans), but wicked spirits (invisible beings) in the spiritual realm.

When we enter a place which is new and unfamiliar to us, we should be ready to rebuke wicked spirits if they are there. But we should also be ready to acknowledge and cooperate with the good spirits which may be there. I have entered homes, churches, and other places, with my spiritual armor ready to do battle, but afterward found it unnecessary. I instead found peaceful, loving and sweet presences.

A whole geographic location can have a special presence of the Lord. The land of Israel is peculiarly anointed of God. The covenants which God has made there over many centuries; the promises and prophecies which God has made concerning Israel, and concerning the Church; the blood of the holy prophets which has been shed there, even the Divine Blood of the Lord Jesus Christ Himself; all of these events have established some things over that land in the realm of the spirit. Angels, anointings, portals, and specific activities are involved there, invisibly, as a result of what God has done, is doing, and shall do there in the future. And we may perceive such things as God would disclose them unto us in a supernatural revelation, or as we pick them up freely by faith.

Why are so many people blessed when they visit Jerusalem to see the land of the Bible? Because they freely open up their hearts by faith to receive a special blessing from the Lord while they are there, and because there are, in fact, special blessings in the realm of the spirit there that can be received.

When walking in the spirit by faith, a person can inwardly sense the Lord wherever he may be at the time. Wherever we go, God is. But it is easier to perceive Him where His anointing is in manifestation in some tangible way. And then it is not simply an *inward* feeling which we would perceive, but it is God's actual presence there in manifestation in some *outward* way.

When we enter a person's home, we may perceive a spiritual presence. The first impression that impacts you when you first enter may be that of the chief spirit (good or evil) that is resident there. Or it may be that of the collective presence of spirit beings as one entity making contact with you. People who have some righteousness and some sins in their lives will have some good spirits and some bad ones in their home at the same time. The more they serve God, the more good spirits will they entertain, and vice versa. If we know what a person's lifestyle is, we can imagine which kinds of spirits he has; or, if we discern those spirits first, then we will know what his lifestyle is.

I enter a house without knowing the owner personally. An invisible presence there greets me somehow and impresses me to praise the Lord. I feel joyful, light, and at peace. The very walls seem to testify of Jesus' lordship there. The plants themselves may seem to shout for joy and also sing. A friend of mine said that her plants began to flourish when she began praying and praising the Lord in their presence.

Some places, items of furniture, or personal things, may have spiritual presences in them, and may be able to speak or make sounds. Through the air conditioner in a church, I once heard many angels singing and playing heavenly music. (It was during a powerfully anointed conference week, so there was obviously a lot of angelic activity going on during those days.) A local print shop owner in my neighborhood told me that both he and his wife (both of whom are Christians) once experienced the same thing in their home: they heard angels singing through an air conditioner. Neither they nor I sought the experience. I think that natural objects, sounds, sights, lights, and even odors, can, at times, become avenues for spiritual ones to be made manifest.

A lot of "things that go 'bump' in the night" may be the activities of spirits in our homes. Not surprisingly, Satan is often the culprit. In the more profound cases, doors or shutters may open and close by themselves, chairs may move, footsteps are heard, items in the home always seem to be getting misplaced, or some other strange thing may occur. If such an experience is inspired by God for some special purpose, it will cause or culminate in a blessing of some kind; if it is not His doing, it will bring an oppression and inconvenience. A lot of our thoughts, feelings, moods, attitudes, lifestyles, behavior, and dreams, may result from the activities of spirits in our homes and lives. A choir of angels in a home can inspire and teach those who live there (without their knowledge) how to praise the Lord, hence the constant singing there.

Animals can also carry spiritual presences. They might behave in a way which is contrary to their nature when there is a strange spirit in them. I once saw a cat behave like a person. An unfriendly cat got angry at me once because I tried to pat him. He got up on his hind legs, walked up to me, grabbed my left leg with his claws, and wrestled with me for a moment the way a little man would. Then he let go and gave me a dirty look as if to say, "Don't mess with me." I was dumbfounded.

I have occasionally prayed for animals, including stray cats and dogs. If they let me, I pick them up and pat them, and pray, "Lord, touch this animal by the anointing of Your precious Holy Spirit. I rebuke any wildness or other kind of negative spirit which he might have in him, and I call him delivered, in Jesus' Name. And Lord, let anyone who sees, touches, or comes into any kind of contact with him, become convicted of his sins and of his need for Jesus, and cry out for his salvation." Animals can be spiritually sensitive and can discern, carry, and cooperate with spirits, and even deal with them, at times.

Think this is farfetched? I once found an injured cat and took him in to help him recover. I also prayed for him and anointed him in the Name of Jesus. I was a new Christian at the time, and did not know very much about spiritual things. As I lay down resting on my living room floor one day, a demonic spirit began bothering me from a wall in front of me. Then that cat came all the way from my room (where he had been asleep only a minute before) jumped onto the edge of a sofa-arm, looked at the demon, and swung his paw at it. The spirit instantly left, and the cat jumped down to the floor and went right back to his room to sleep.

The way the cat hit the floor and walked away was so pointed (as if to say to the spirit, "Don't mess with my master!"), I know he knew what had just occurred. Again, I was dumbfounded. That cat had been led by the Holy Spirit to rebuke that oppressor.

Animals can sometimes perceive and respond to spiritual presences. Don't your pets occasionally help you discern who you're with? On a television talk show, a man once let his dog pick out a date for him from the audience. He really did seem to make a good choice—the very one I'd guessed and hoped he would. Of course, we shouldn't depend on their judgment. Animals are of a lower order of being.

There are, it may be, so many kinds of voices, noises, and presences in the world, and so many kinds of beings, places, and things through which they can be manifested. Spirits are not in everybody or in everything, and those which are may or may not be of God. It is when the Holy Spirit is present somewhere, or in someone or something, that we want to welcome Him and not resist Him, receive and not grieve Him. He may be there for a special reason.

In this book, I am endeavoring to encourage our faith in this area because God manifests Himself here and, therefore, we can find Him here. It is true that for a lack of wisdom (Hosea 4:6a), many people have been deceived by evil spirits manifesting themselves in voices, noises, and presences which they erroneously gave themselves over to.[1] There are false prophets, spiritists, and people in insane asylums, who have been misled by voices and other kinds of spiritual manifestations which they did not properly discern, and did not know how to resist. But if Satan can work in these ways, it is only because God opened up that realm in the beginning for His own use. Every false prophet, false religion, and false teaching, contains some elements of truth which have been perverted by Satan in his efforts to deceive and mislead people.

The devil is a liar, (John 8:44). He comes to trap men and take them captive at his will (2Timothy 2:26), to devour them as a roaring lion (1Peter 5:8), and to otherwise steal, kill, and destroy them, (John 10:10). Many of his tactics involve supernatural powers because he knows that they affect people and captivate them in a compelling way. People want to have supernatural power, so when Satan offers it to them, they are often willing to sell their souls for it. But if we will remain sober and vigilant in the Word of God, and constant in prayer, we will be able to recognize the enemy when he comes on the scene, and not be moved or deceived by him. We are to stand against the wiles of the enemy and not be ignorant of his devices, (Ephesians 6:11; 2Corinthians 2:11).

When we walk in the spirit, we will find that we cannot say "Amen" to everything we hear, and that not everyone who names the Name of Christ or says "Praise the Lord, God bless you" is of God. We will also be able to control ourselves, and not become easily excited at the manifestation of spiritual presences, even if they are of God. Yes, we should enjoy the presence of the Lord in our church services, but our joy need not be expressly unbridled.

There is an appropriate time for expressing ourselves freely before the Lord, but there is also a need to remain alert and watchful in the spirit so that spiritual enemies won't creep into the service.

As we train ourselves to discern between good and evil, we are going to realize that the inner witness of the spirit plays a crucial role. The born-again human spirit, which is anointed with the presence of the Holy Spirit of God, and which has the mind of Christ, is a trustworthy source of communication from God. When He speaks to us in a supernatural way, it is more clear than His simple revelations and, therefore, more desirable. But He doesn't speak to us supernaturally all the time, as He does in simple ways. So we need to get to know our own spirit (which has been recreated into the image of Christ; Colossians 3:10), get to know the Holy Spirit, and learn to understand their diverse communications.

1Thessalonians 5:19-23a   Quench not the Spirit. Despise not prophesyings. Prove all things; hold fast that which is good. Abstain from all appearance of evil. And the very God of peace sanctify you wholly.

Our spirit does not want to quench the Holy Spirit. He does not despise prophesyings, visions, miracles, and other supernatural manifestations. He knows how to prove all things, how to hold firmly to that which is good, that which is of God, and how to reject all that is evil. He knows that when something is of God, His anointing sanctifies and blesses him wholly; and when something is not of God, it doesn't. Our spirit is made strong and full of faith when we gain knowledge, wisdom, and spiritual discernment, in any area. Then we can fearlessly walk on those waters when the Lord bids us, "It is I, come."

Revelation 4:1-2 After this I looked, and behold, a door was opened in

heaven: and the first voice which I heard was as it were of a trumpet talking with me; which said, Come up hither, and I will shew thee things which must be hereafter. And immediately I was in the spirit: and, behold, a Throne was set in Heaven, and One sat on the Throne.

In this *open heaven* vision, John sees a door standing open in the sky (the *first heaven,* our *atmosphere).* Then the same familiar Voice which gave him the messages for the seven churches, again speaks to him. Jesus summons him, "Come up Here," and John goes flying out of his body (in an *out-of-body experience),* through that door, past the *second heaven (outer space),* and into the *Third Heaven* (the *Paradise of God;* 2Corinthians 12:9), in a *heavenly visitation* vision.

Had Jesus not preceded His summons to "Come up Hither" with the visions and revelations in chapters 1-3, John might have hesitated to quickly leave his body and fly out of the earth realm, and that would have limited what the Lord wanted to do. But those first seven revelations blessed and sanctified him wholly, and the increasingly familiar voice of Jesus made him feel increasingly comfortable as it called him to ascend to higher realms.

In our natural lives, the Lord manifests Himself to us gradually, blessing us, teaching us, anointing us progressively from glory to glory as we become more and more familiar with Him. In our supernatural experiences as well, He often manifests Himself gradually so that we will become more and more familiar and comfortable with Him and with that realm. Then we won't draw back and limit Him when He calls us to walk with Him there.

Endnotes

[1]   In November, 1994, I dreamed that many people who had consulted psychic mediums, astrologers, and spiritists, were seeking deliverance from the devil's torments. By having entertained evil spirits, they had opened the door to the devil and were hearing his voice and becoming controlled by him, and they were helpless to resist him. The Holy Spirit showed me the word "voices" to indicate to me that that's the way the devil was oppressing them— through a variety of evil voices in the spiritual realm. That's why we must beware the voices we seek to hear from.

So these people began to acknowledge their need for a supernatural deliverance, and were asking God in their hearts, "Where can I go and to whom can I turn and what must I do to be saved?" As I saw these people in this dream, I was thinking to myself, "Hey, I can help them. I've got the answer. I know the Truth (Jesus), and I have written about these things." Then I thought to myself, "How appropriate my books are for such a time as this," and reviewed some of my titles, including this particular one, which I trust is addressing this subject competently and helping those who desire to come to the knowledge of the Truth, so that the Truth can make them free, (John 8:32). Then I awoke.

Beware of those false prophets who come to you in sheep's clothing but inwardly are ravening wolves possessed by devils seeking whom they may devour. Seek Jesus and the Word of God and be instructed and led by His precious Spirit, and give attention only to those servants and handmaids of God who are truly anointed of Him. And if you're not sure if someone is really of God, ask Him to give you discernment so that you can "test the spirits whether they are of God," (1John 4:1).

Chapter 6

PORTALS, PATHWAYS, & STRUCTURES

Hebrews 8:1-2 Now of the things which we have spoken this is the sum: We have such an High Priest, Who is set on the right hand of the Throne of the Majesty in the heavens; A Minister of the Sanctuary, and of the True Tabernacle, which the Lord pitched, and not man.

The Patriarch Moses spoke of a *True Tabernacle* which the Lord Himself pitched, and which served as his pattern for the Tabernacle in the wilderness, (Hebrews 8:5). The Prophet Ezekiel spoke of the *portals* and of the *inner chambers* which he saw in that Heavenly Sanctuary, (Ezekiel 40-48). And the Prophet Malachi spoke of the *windows* of Heaven, (Malachi 3:10). The City of God in the Third Heaven, though invisible, is real. The first and second heavens (our atmospheric sky and outer space, respectively) also contain invisible structures in specific locations, and they, too, may have openings by which one can enter into another realm. *Black holes* in outer space prove this, even though they only represent a lower order of heavenly portals.

A medical missionary to South America, Dr. Percy Collett, experienced a powerful heavenly visitation for 5½ days, during which time the Lord gave him a prophetic message for the last days and many insights about the supernatural realm. That was over three decades ago. He testifies that while he was in Heaven talking with Jesus, the Lord taught him that when Christians die they go through a certain invisible pathway in the sky over Sweden. Wherever they may be at the time, that is the route the angels use as they take them out of the earth and on their way to Heaven.

This missionary also learned that there is a certain area within our atmosphere which is the specific location of the spiritual door to Hades (Hell).

Within that area, commonly known as the Bermuda Triangle, there is an invisible portal in the sky, and when people die without Christ, wherever they may be on earth at the time, they take that route out of here and enter that Abode of the Lost. Another minister saw that when people die they are first brought by angels before the Book of Life (Revelation 20:11-15) to see whether their name is written in it; then they are directed accordingly.

If these reports are true, they show that the invisible realm is not all chaos. There is still order in the universe. Though man was separated from God through Adam's sin, we are not completely severed from contact with Him. In Him we still live and move and have our being, (Acts 17:28). The earth, too, still interacts with the heavens, does business with them, and permits communication and transportation in them.

Most people are kept from doing heavenly business because of sin and natural-mindedness. But when we are in right standing with God, and become spiritually-minded, it is easier to perceive the things which are Above and set our affection on them, as the Apostle Paul exhorts us to do, (Colossians 3:1). We will have confidence to come before God's Throne of Grace when we have clean hands and a pure heart.

Psalms 24:3-4 Who shall ascend into the hill of the Lord? or who shall stand in His Holy Place? He that hath clean hands, and a pure heart; who hath not lifted up his soul unto vanity, nor sworn deceitfully.

Our God is in the heavens (Psalms 115:3), and He discloses divinely inspired ideas to good men with good intentions as they approach Him. I'm sure that the great Scientist Albert Einstein saw some of the same mathematical equations that I once saw as I flew heavenward in an out-of-body experience—only he knew how to use them for earthly good because he understood the mathematical sciences.

Our Lord spoke of the *keys* of the Kingdom of Heaven—to *bind,* to *loose,* to *close,* to *open,* both earthly things and heavenly things, (Matthew 18:18). The Prophet Elijah was given the *key* to loosen fire from the sky, (2Kings 1:10). And the Apostle Peter was given the *keys* of the Kingdom of Heaven so that whatsoever he would decree would come to pass, (Matthew 16:19).

The authorities and powers given to the Body of Christ involve both human and angelic beings, and both earthly and heavenly realms. A lot of what God's servants decree through prayer determines how things—natural and supernatural—will turn out. I once dreamed that Prophet Morris Cerullo had the ability (the *anointing,* the *key),* to be able to pray for a person to experience a trance, a heavenly visitation, or another type of vision, and it would come to pass.

In an out-of-body experience, I saw Pastor Elcio Salgado, and his wife, and they were encouraging me to step over a threshold in a portal in the sky in order to step into a new spiritual dimension, a higher realm than I had ever known before. I knew it was the Lord's bidding, "Come up higher," but I hesitated at first because it was new and unfamiliar to me, until I saw the pastor and his wife, both of whom I knew and trusted, encouraging me in this vision. So I stepped over into that new realm which the Lord was disclosing unto me, and received a new anointing *there.*

We are not alone. Although in the natural we may be alone at times, in the realm of the spirit we are surrounded with angels, anointings, pathways, and portals. Many voices and sounds we hear, sights we see, and presences we perceive in the supernatural realm, involve a combination of several of these. John saw a door opened in the sky, heard the audible voice of Jesus, went through that door, and entered a higher dimension in the realm of the spirit, (Revelation 4:1-2). Then he was able to behold the Throne of God and other divine marvels in the Third Heaven.

We will not experience these kinds of things each time that we enter the spiritual realm. But it is good to know what is there so that if they would come into our view, they will not be strange to us. A basic, biblical knowledge of what is in the spiritual realm will help us enter it with confidence and receive the fullness of what God would disclose to us from there in a supernatural experience. Even so, most visions involve only a small number of activities, and short, simple messages.

When we still our natural senses for a moment and ask the Lord if there is something He is trying to disclose to us, He may answer us in a number of ways: by an inner witness, a voice, a vision, etc. He may simply tell us He is with us in a general way and is not disclosing anything specific at that time. But if He is, opening up to Him by faith will help His gentle, easily grievable Spirit to begin disclosing. Small beginnings can end in great revelations.

It should not be a strange idea to us that God can require the cooperation of our faith when He wants to manifest Himself to us in a supernatural way. Even in sovereign moves of His Spirit, it is impossible to please God without faith, (Hebrews 11:6). As we observed in Chapter 1, in the context of the initial outpouring of the Holy Spirit on the Day of Pentecost (Acts 2:1-4), the 120 disciples in the Upper Room were sovereignly visited by the Holy Ghost. But their faith, knowledge, and yieldedness, played a major role in that visitation. God moved when they met His conditions.

Before the supernatural manifestation came, they had been studying the Word of God, fasting, and praying with faith in what Jesus had promised them. When the promise of the Spirit came, they were in one accord and fully yielded. And when the Spirit led them to go outside and preach the Gospel and set the captives free, they continued to cooperate with Him in every conceivable and practical way.

The great Pentecostal revival at Azusa Street, in Los Angeles, California, in 1906, was a sovereign visitation of the Holy Ghost. But those Christians upon whom the Spirit first descended there also had to yield to Him by faith.

Supernatural though it was, their initial baptism in the Holy Spirit with the biblical evidence of speaking with other tongues occurred only after the first recipient had been shown in a vision "how to" speak with tongues.

God didn't make those Pentecostal pioneers speak with tongues (as many Christians would like to believe, and would like God to do to them). Yes, there were many spontaneous burstings forth of utterances in tongues among them, as there are among us today. But they were preceded by a practical teaching with which they had to cooperate, as it is with us today. In his vision, Brother Edward Lee saw Christ's apostles teaching him how to speak with tongues. As a result of this practical instruction, he received the fullness of the Holy Spirit and was instrumental in leading many others into this experience in the early stages of the groundbreaking Azusa Street revival.

Today, too, there are many manifestations of the Holy Spirit in our midst, even sovereign ones. But they normally occur according to what we believe Him for, and we can only believe Him for what we have studied and prepared ourselves. The Kingdom of Heaven permits us—yes, encourages us—to take those things which are Above by force, by pressing into the spiritual realm and seizing them by faith, (Matthew 11:12). According to our faith, and God's permission, it will be done unto us, (Matthew 9:29).

In my own experience, I have found that practical teaching has usually been the key to receiving anointings from God. In July, 1982, I read Kenneth E. Hagin's book, *Seven Steps to Receiving the Holy Spirit,* embraced the knowledge there, cooperated with the Holy Spirit's desire to fill me, fasted for 13 days, and received the Holy Spirit on the day after I ended the fast, under the anointing of Gloria Copeland's Bible teaching in the Tarrant County Convention Center, Fort Worth, Texas. I credit the experience with my ability to cooperate with it. My faith to receive it was enhanced by my new knowledge about it. Faith comes by hearing, reading, and otherwise apprehending the Word of God, (Romans 10:17).

The audible voice of God visited me in 2001, but He was forced to redefine it. I worked as temporary office personnel in the office of Koji Nakanishi, one of the world's foremost organic chemists, at Columbia University, here in New York. While there for a few weeks I walked around the campus and inquired about the possibility of studying there. Nothing serious, but I was very impressed with the school and secretly wished I could study there. That was between September and October, 2000. I didn't give it more thought after that, and basically just forgot about it.

Then in February 2001, I was awakened by the audible voice of God. He simply said, "Go to Columbia." I was both startled and amused. After some giggling and chatting with the Lord, I said, "You want to go to Columbia? Okay, let's go to Columbia University," and made the first call there requesting their application packet. Although I received a number of confirmations affirming the endeavor, and felt anointed about it all the way through the process of applying, being interviewed, taking their campus tour, and sitting in a couple of classes, I thought I'd research some other schools just in case Columbia declines my application.

A month later, in March, I heard His voice again: "I said Columbia!" I was shaken. I thought God must really have something important in store in me going to Columbia University if He's going to guide me like that. What awesome things must He have in store?! Then in April, they declined my application, and that really depressed me for a few weeks. I didn't doubt Him or His leading, but found it hard to understand why it didn't come to pass as He had wished, seeing He was so forceful in the leading. Then in May, He sent an angel in a dream and told me I could do whatever I want. I chose The Katharine Gibbs School, New York, and had a great experience there. It changed my life and outlook. During the Associate in Applied Sciences degree program, He spoke clearly in my mind one day, and said, "This is your Columbia." He counted my Gibbs experience as if it was at Columbia.

For the supernatural dreams, visions, and revelations that I receive from the Lord, I also must give much credit to the understanding He's given me about these kinds of experiences. It is largely for knowing how to yield to his presence that I have come to experience it.

Sometimes we can determine which kind of presence will manifest in a supernatural experience. The particular kind of anointing of the Holy Spirit which we've been asking of God may be just what is disclosed at the time of His visitation unto us. Pastor Benny Hinn has come to know the Holy Spirit in an intimate way, and has learned how to minister to people by His leading, because he specifically asked in prayer, "Holy Spirit, I want to know You." He shares his wonderful testimony in his book, *The Anointing.*

Our prayers, our acts, and our faith can hasten spiritual activity. By taking Holy Communion in our private time before the Lord, by anointing ourselves with holy oil, by seeking the Face of God, by calling upon the power of God, or by doing similar kinds of spiritual exercises, a great many kinds of presences from God can manifest. And, obviously, if we don't do these things, His various anointings are not likely to manifest at all.

One of the most wonderful experiences which I have ever had in the supernatural presence of God occurred because of something which I initiated. The idea came to me to totally clean up my room, shave, shower, and dress up with a brand new shirt which I'd been saving for a special occasion—then go to private prayer. Well, when I started praying, it seemed as if the Spirit of God was really excited and anxious to fellowship with me, and as if the angels, too, were anticipating my praying, as if they had been looking forward to it. Jesus Himself seemed to be smiling and ready to be with me.

Even though I didn't see any of this in a vision, I felt like that was the reality. I think that that reality came about because of what I'd established in my heart—to prepare the way of the Lord by sanctifying myself and my room. This is why I believe that our prayers, our acts and our faith, coming from pure motives, can hasten spiritual activity and inspire God's anointing to show up. However, we should not seek supernaturals for their own sake but simply seek the Lord; seek the Giver, not the gifts—the Blesser, not the blessings. If He discloses supernaturals, fine—if not, fine—but we have Him, nonetheless, all the time.

The Lord has many things that He'd like to disclose, but many times He cannot speak to us as unto spiritual adults, but as children. We cannot bear most of what He would like to reveal, (Hebrews 5:14). But when He comes slowly, perhaps with a simple presence, an angelic song, or a pleasant vision, then we will be more inclined to recognize and yield to Him. Then He might feed us "stronger meat."

Eliphaz became afraid when an angel visited him with a revelation from the Lord, therefore he only received *a little thereof,* (Job 4:12-21). Ezekiel, being a Prophet of God, and more experienced in supernatural manifestations, was fully given to disclosings from the Lord, (Ezekiel 1:1). The Body of Christ today is more anointed and experienced than Ezekiel was, and can, therefore, receive even greater revelations than he had. Jesus Himself said that greater things than these shall the Body of Christ do, (John 14:12).

The Lord needs to disclose some great revelations unto us, so He will give us great faith, discernment, and skill to yield to them. Heavenly revelations are often hidden behind and preceded by subtle voices, noises, and presences, which we must know how to yield to if we would receive the fullness thereof.

Chapter 7

ASK WISDOM

Proverbs 1:20   Wisdom crieth without; she uttereth her voice in the streets.

With all the yielding to the Holy Spirit which we want and need to do, we need wisdom from God. The prophets in the Bible who received astounding revelations from God were not "more" people, people who were always asking God for more and more of His anointing. It is a legitimate and divinely appointed desire which God has given us in these days to ask for more and more of His presence, but it doesn't invalidate the need to ask for wisdom the way the prophets of old did to prepare for the manifestation of the Spirit.

Wisdom is so accessible and easy to receive that no one is excused for doing without her. She is a precious person from God and goes out of her way—literally into the streets where people do business—crying out for whosoever will have ears to hear to receive her guidance. At the start of any endeavor, any fresh anointing or new beginning, wisdom ought to go before us. King Solomon asked wisdom at the beginning of his reign and received everything he didn't ask for alongside her. God Himself employed her before even beginning to lay the foundations of the earth, (Proverbs 8:22-30). If we, too, will love her, she will cause us to inherit substance, whether material substance or the substance of the anointings of God, (Proverbs 8:21).

Matthew 7:7-8   Ask, and it shall be given you; seek, and ye shall find; knock, and it shall be opened unto you: For every one that asketh receiveth; and he that seeketh findeth; and to him that knocketh it shall be opened.

Matthew 9:29-30a Then touched He their eyes, saying, According to your faith be it unto you. And their eyes were opened.

The realm of the spirit is being disclosed as never before in these last days, particularly now that there is a new anointing in the earth. It almost seems as if anyone who asks, whosoever will, may enter in and take some anointings from the atmosphere because they are being so freely and graciously given. Whereas it has always been that one would have to pay a price in prayer and spiritual exercises for years before they could receive certain giftings—exercises which are important and not to be neglected, even today—the realm of God's giftings are unbelievably accessible now more than ever because of the uniqueness of the present time.

We are living in times of refreshing. This is the season of the favor of the Lord and God is pouring out His blessings and giftings freely and profusely, even to those who haven't necessarily "paid a price" for them. Someone else may have paid the price for them.

People who are just now getting saved and receiving prayer ministry are receiving the Holy Spirit and His diverse gifts more quickly than new converts throughout history. They're receiving more because God is giving more in this season and imparting unto this generation a divinely appointed desire and faith to ask and receive more. The older generation can also receive more because it is for this reason that they've paid what price they may have paid: they have been made ready for just such a time as this.

Since the spiritual atmosphere around the world is so graciously open and giving gifts, it is so easy now to ask and receive dreams, visions, and revelations of the Lord. One of the most common prayers we hear from ministers and ministry team members as they pray for people is, "Lord, give him more dreams, more visions, more revelations of Your Spirit. Let her hear Your voice. Open his spiritual senses to be able to see in the spirit." Now this is not an inappropriate prayer. It is a good prayer, and I myself pray like this for people sometimes. But I think we are too quick sometimes to pray or prophesy for someone to see in the realm of the spirit.

Not everyone needs to see or discern profound things in the realm of the spirit. Although the anointing would give people this ability, it is not always advantageous, and it is not always fun. Many people are not ready for the profounder things of the Spirit, but they may yet apprehend them when there comes an outpouring of God. God does not always check carefully to see who is mature enough to receive His gifts when He sends a collective disclosing of His Spirit. Jesus said, "Everyone that asks receives." Once a person begins to ask, seek and knock, there can begin to be such things disclosed unto him as he is desiring, whether or not he is ready for them. This is why we caution people, "Be careful what you pray for—you just might get it!" So I think we ought to try and be soberminded when asking for certain giftings of the Holy Spirit—particularly the revelation gifts—because once they're given, they're in us to stay.

A friend of mine from the handball courts of Williamsburg, Brooklyn, told me he'd like to be able to see in the spirit like I do, and even more keenly. I told him what I often tell people, "You don't know what you're asking for. It isn't always the blessing one would think or hope. You don't know how blessed you are to be normal instead of supernormal." This brother is not even a dedicated Christian, and he's already wishing he had supernatural powers. I understood quickly, from what he described to me, that he was asking from a purely selfish motive.

There are times that experiencing the supernatural and seeing into the realm of the spirit is a glorious ecstatic experience, as when an angel appears, when Jesus speaks audibly, or when one sees a marvelous vision of Heaven. There are many times, too, that it is not at all fun. I've had the feeling of regret at being able to see and hear in the spirit many times. When prayer has been made for me that I would "get more dreams and visions," I have, at times, wished for less instead.

Some prophetic individuals have gone as far as to say that their gifting is as often like a curse as it is a blessing because of the severity and seriousness of the things they are permitted to behold. Nevertheless, even after experiencing oftentimes displeasure at some manifestations of the Holy Spirit, I never really regret having this anointing. It is Jesus, and howsoever He is pleased to use me for His glory is totally cool with me.

If I, being chosen and anointed to walk in this kind of anointing, can be caused to almost regret accepting it, then certainly those who are not called to it ought to consider carefully what they should and should not pray for. Recently, I began asking people if they want to have more dreams and visions and hear God speak to them more distinctly before praying for them to receive such revelations; and I tell people it's okay and they should not feel guilty if they decline.

Given all this, in my experienced opinion, I would advise a true devotion to the Lord and a sincere commitment to the study of the Bible to anyone seeking the things which are Above. And if a person has had a history in the occult and has any unresolved issues with evil visions, voices or presences, he surely should seek a healing from God before ministering unto others with revelation gifts.

Although we can find many exceptions nowadays, our rule should be that several years of walking closely with the Lord ought to transpire before one begins to operate in the profounder anointings of revelation. One ought to walk by faith for a season and learn about the precious gifts of the Holy Spirit in preparation and anticipation of their soon coming unto him. Then he shall have faith for these things and, in God's own time and way, he can receive a special impartation of them. Then he can ask and they shall be given unto him; he can both seek and find them; when he knocks, this door shall be opened unto him.

Chapter 8

PRAYERS

Supernatural manifestations of voices, noises and presences, are not going to be experienced by everyone, and those who do experience them will not necessarily experience them often. In addition, when such things are manifested, they may come by God's own hand directly disclosing them without our having asked or prepared for them. In such cases, our own faith, knowledge and will, may not be required as much because God's Spirit is working superiorly to them. God is in control, and He often arrests and lords over our souls in supernatural experiences.

Yet, in many cases, our own faith, knowledge and will, do indeed figure in the kind of supernatural manifestation we will experience, and may also determine the extent of it. Even when God directly initiates a supernatural manifestation because He has a particular purpose in mind, He will usually permit and look for our cooperation with the visitation of His Spirit, even though it may not be required. It is then that we should have faith for the supernatural, a practical knowledge of supernatural things, and a willingness to yield to them.

To the end that we will become conducive to the supernatural doings of the Lord, a right relationship with Him and right thinking are prerequisite. The following prayers may assist us in this. Pray these prayers, and trust God to work in you a full salvation experience, and a complete deliverance from evil things. Also trust Him to anoint you with spiritual sensitivity and discernment, by which you will be able to know when something is happening in the spiritual realm, what it is that's happening, and how you should respond.

Prayer for Salvation

John 3:16 For God so loved the world, that He gave His only begotten Son, that whosoever believeth in Him should not perish, but have everlasting life.

"Oh Lord God, I come to You in the precious Name of Jesus, and repent of my sins. Please have mercy on me, forgive me, and wash me in the Holy Blood of Jesus. I believe that Jesus Christ died for my sins and was raised from the dead for my justification, and I accept Him into my heart right now, to be my personal Lord and Savior. I trust You to take out of my life anything that is not pleasing to You, anything that is not according to Your Holy Word.

"Fill me with the power of Your mighty Holy Spirit, and transform me into the kind of person You want me to be. I'm saved now, through faith in Jesus Christ. I belong to You, Lord God, and I commit myself completely to Your will. I will pray, I will read the Bible, I will go to church, and I will serve You in every and any way You want me to. Have Your way in my life, completely, and use me for Your glory. In the Name of Jesus. Amen."

---

sign your name and date here, and as you do so, believe, by faith, that it is also being written in the Lamb's (Jesus) Book of Life in Heaven, (Revelation 20:11-15).

Prayer for Deliverance

Isaiah 10:27 And it shall come to pass in that day, that his burden shall be taken away from off thy shoulder, and his yoke from off thy neck, and the yoke shall be destroyed because of the anointing.

"God, I need Your help. I've been experiencing evil voices, noises, presences, nightmares, and similar kinds of spiritual disturbances. I ask You to remove all these things from my life, my home, and my family, and show me if there are any inappropriate items which You want me to get rid of. Deliver me from all those evil things by the power of Your Holy Spirit, the precious Blood of Jesus, the Word of God, and by the ministry of Your holy angels. In Jesus' Name.

"In a supernatural way, visit my life with Your light, Lord, and dispel every force of darkness. Cast out every evil spirit that has been bothering me, and protect me with Your whole armor. Let Your angels go with me wherever I go, and help me in everything I do. Let no trick of the enemy prosper against me, but give me victory in every spiritual battle. In the Name of Jesus. Amen."

Prayer for Discernment

1John 4:1 Beloved, believe not every spirit, but try the spirits whether they are of God: because many false prophets are gone out into the world.

"Lord, I ask You to anoint me with Your Holy Spirit in a special way right now. Enable me to understand spiritual things. Voices, noises, presences, and other spiritual manifestations, may or may not be from You, and I need to be able to tell the difference. I need to know how to test the spirits whether they are of You.

"As I study Your Word concerning all these things, and pray, and stay in Your will, I trust You to teach me to win in spiritual warfare against evil manifestations, and I believe You will give me keen spiritual perception, discernment, and sensitivity. This way I'll know when a spirit is manifesting, whether or not it's of You, and how to respond to it. I do not want to miss any visitation of You, Lord God, howsoever it may come.

"In all these things, as in every other area of my life also, I trust in the lordship of Your Holy Spirit, and I rest in Him. In the Name of Jesus. Amen."

Books by David A. Castro

Understanding Supernatural Dreams According to the Bible
A Living Classic, $24.95

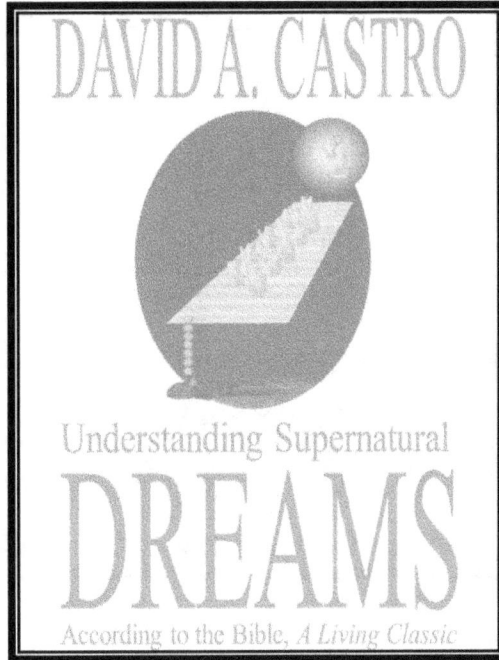

A profoundly spiritual, strictly biblical work, this expository reference book may be considered "required reading" for students of the Spirit. It takes the reader on into the spiritual realm and examines dreams therefrom. A classic in its field, it offers to help the reader understand the broad spectrum of dreams and dreaming, and may assist in healing and deliverance from sleep/dream problems. It provides many practical guidelines on trances, audible voices, out-of-body experiences, and other kinds of visions, and encourages the Body of Christ to yield to the Holy Spirit for supernatural experiences along these lines. Highly Recommended.

Chapters include: What is a Dream?; Be Renewed in the Spirit of Your Dream Life; Sleep in Heavenly Peace; Adventures in the Night Seasons; Dream Recall and Interpretation; Try the Dreams Whether they are of God; Some Experiences; Supernatural Dreams and Trances; Endtime Dreamers; Glossary; 254 pages; 8¼ x 10½"

Understanding Supernatural Visions According to the Bible
$19.95

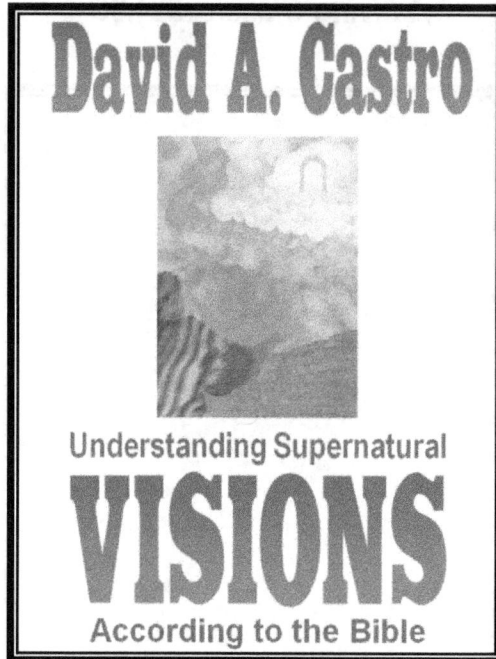

Explores a variety of different kinds of visions and clarifies many issues involved in the various realms of supernatural revelations. It encourages Christians to seek those things which are Above (Colossians 3:1), while at the same time challenges us to gain a foundation in the Word of God, to check the motives of our own hearts, and to walk in the anointing of the Holy Spirit with Jesus. It is profoundly insightful and helpful to prophets, intercessors, and others who receive visions and revelations of the Lord.

Chapters include: Spiritual Vision; Pictorial Vision; Panoramic Vision; Dream (Night Vision); Audible Message; Apparition; Divine Sight; Open Heaven; Trance; Out-of-body Experience; Translation; Heavenly Visitation; Wisdom is the Principal Thing; Glossary; 100 pages; 8¼ x 10½"

Understanding Voices, Noises & Presences in the Spiritual Realm, $14.95

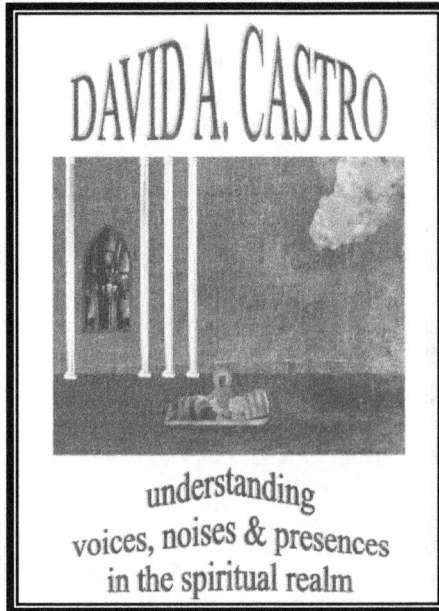

In this unique booklet, David addresses spiritual and mystical experiences in a refreshingly insightful manner. As always, he teaches strictly from the Bible as he shines new light on the subject of the spiritual realm and its various manifestations. He shows how to discern which experiences are of God, and endeavors to remove fear and impart faith for supernatural experiences which are of Him.

Chapters include: Yield to the Spirit; Peculiar Disclosings; Angelic Involvement; Spiritual Presences Around People; Spiritual Presences in Certain Places; Portals, Pathways and Structures; Ask Wisdom; Prayers; 74 pages; 7 x 10"

The Supernatural Ministry of Angels
$14.95

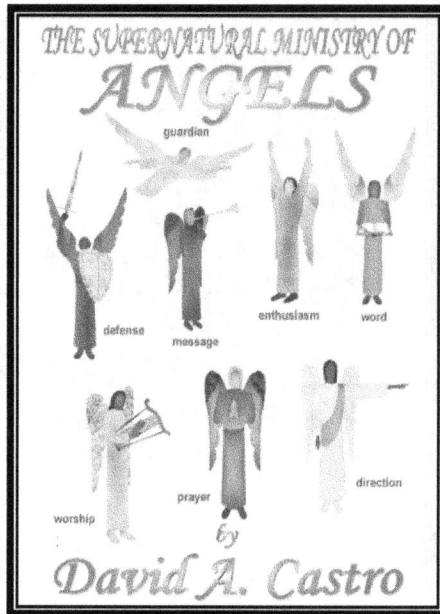

A thorough yet concise study on the ministry of angels according to the Bible. No mythical, fancy ideas or popular notions are given, but a truly scriptural observation and general analysis of the entire spectrum of angels. 30 questions about angels and their personal, practical involvement in our lives are answered, and where the Scripture is silent or unclear, qualified opinion is given.

Chapters include: A Prophecy; Kinds of Angels; Jesus, Lord of Angels; Angelic Fellow-Servants; Angels Unawares; Angelic Providence; Evil Angels; Serving God Releases Angels; Tongues of Angels; 30 Questions & Answers; includes a General Listing of Angelic Orders and Employments; 74 pages; 7 x 10"

Understanding Supernatural Experiences According to the Bible
$24.95

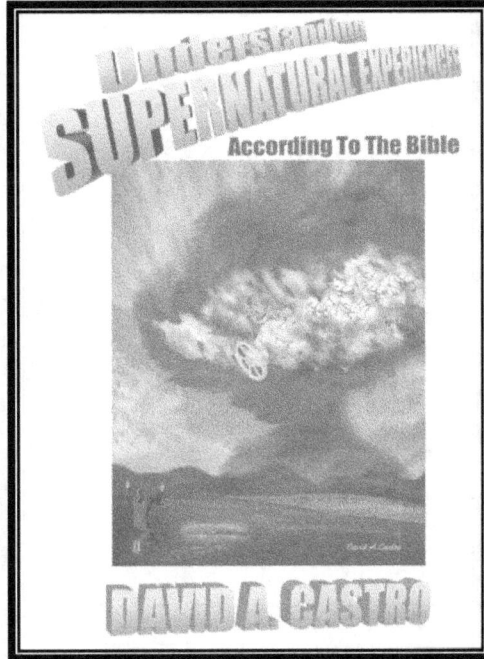

Over twenty years in the making, this extraordinary writing reveals how the supernatural realm works, what the Holy Spirit is able to do, and encourages God's people to embrace the supernatural dimensions of the anointing. Signs and wonders in the heavens and in the earth—revival, special anointings and the Shekinah Glory, trances, stigmata and levitation—are all explained.

Chapters include: Seek the Things Above; My Personal Testimony; The Power of Revelations; Now Concerning Supernaturals; Kinds of Supernatural Experiences; Special Anointings; Understanding the Anointing; Judging Supernatural Experiences; History of Signs and Wonders; Prepare Ye the Way of the Lord; 184 pages; 8¼ x 10½"

30 Years of Dreams Visions Trances
$14.95

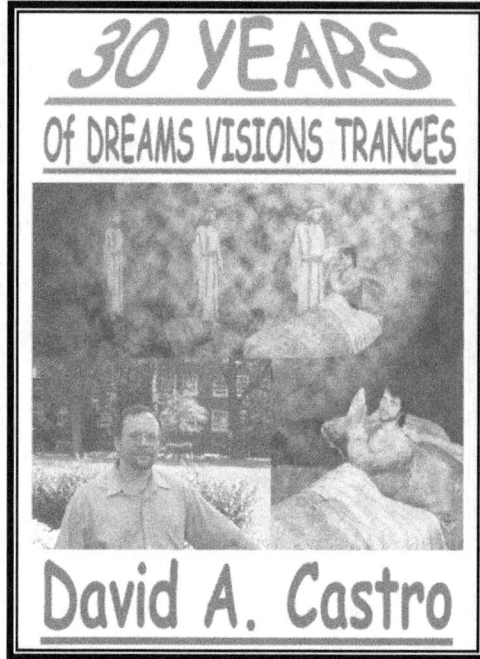

Here David shares a number of supernatural experiences that he has had from the time of his conversion in 1979, in Honolulu, Hawaii. In a wide range of dreams, visions, trances, angelic encounters, and manifestations of the voice of God, he has come to understand their dynamic functions, and hopes to impart wisdom and anointing to the reader through the sharing of the experiences.

Chapters include: Shekinah Glory; Family History; How I Became Christian; I Want to Serve God; How God Speaks in Visions; 74 pages; 7 x 10"

Please order online from www.Amazon.com

Order Form Sample			
Qty	Title	Each	Price
	Understanding Supernatural Dreams According to the Bible, *A Living Classic*	$24.95	
	Understanding Supernatural Visions According to the Bible	$19.95	
	Understanding Voices, Noises & Presences in the Spiritual Realm	$14.95	
	The Supernatural Ministry of Angels	$14.95	
	Understanding Supernatural Experiences According to the Bible	$24.95	
	30 Years of Dreams Visions Trances	$14.95	
		SubTotal	
		S & H	
		Total	

UNDERSTANDING VOICES, NOISES & PRESENCES IN THE SPIRITUAL REALM

80 03

www.brooklynblessing.com

www.twitter.com/daword

www.ingramcontent.com/pod-product-compliance
Lightning Source LLC
LaVergne TN
LVHW061229060426
835509LV00012B/1472